VOCAL SOLO VOLUMES 1 AND 2 COMPLETE

Kids' Musical Theatre Collection

Kids' Musical Theatre Collection

Technicolor® is the registered trademark of the Technicolor group of companies.

ISBN 978-1-4803-6728-9

HAL•LEONARD®
CORPORATION
7777 W. BLUEMOUND RD. P.O. BOX 13819 MILWAUKEE, WI 53213

For all works contained herein:
Unauthorized copying, arranging, adapting, recording, Internet posting, public performance,
or other distribution of the printed music in this publication is an infringement of copyright.
Infringers are liable under the law.

Visit Hal Leonard Online at
www.halleonard.com

TABLE OF CONTENTS

PAGE	TITLE	SHOW/FILM
4	Any Dream Will Do	*Joseph and the Amazing Technicolor® Dreamcoat*
10	Baby Mine	*Dumbo*
14	Be Kind to Your Parents	*Fanny*
18	Bein' Green	*Sesame Street*
22	Born to Entertain	*Ruthless*
30	The Candy Man	*Willy Wonka and the Chocolate Factory*
27	Castle on a Cloud	*Les Misérables*
34	Consider Yourself	*Oliver!*
38	Cruella de Vil	*101 Dalmatians*
44	Dream for Your Inspiration	*The Muppets Take Manhattan*
41	Ev'rybody Wants to be a Cat	*The Aristocats*
52	Feed the Birds	*Mary Poppins*
49	Friend	*Snoopy!!*
57	Gary, Indiana	*The Music Man*
60	Getting to Know You	*The King and I*
64	God Help the Outcasts	*The Hunchback of Notre Dame*
71	Happiness	*You're a Good Man, Charlie Brown*
74	I Always Knew	*Annie Warbucks*
77	I Don't Need Anything but You	*Annie*
82	I Don't Want to Live on the Moon	*Sesame Street*
91	I Got the Sun in the Morning	*Annie Get Your Gun*
86	I Know Things Now	*Into the Woods*
102	I Whistle a Happy Tune	*The King and I*
96	I Won't Grow Up	*Peter Pan*
107	I'd Do Anything	*Oliver!*
110	I'm Late	*Alice in Wonderland*
112	I've Got No Strings	*Pinocchio*
114	In My Own Little Corner	*Cinderella*
118	It's the Hard-Knock Life	*Annie*
122	Join the Circus	*Barnum*

PAGE	TITLE	SHOW/FILM
126	Les Poissons	*The Little Mermaid*
131	Let Me Entertain You	*Gypsy*
134	Let's Go Fly a Kite	*Mary Poppins*
137	Little Lamb	*Gypsy*
140	Little People	*Les Misérables*
145	Maybe	*Annie*
148	My Best Girl (My Best Beau)	*Mame*
154	My Favorite Things	*The Sound of Music*
151	On the Good Ship Lollipop	*Bright Eyes*
158	Part of Your World	*The Little Mermaid*
165	Put on a Happy Face	*Bye Bye Birdie*
168	Real Live Girl	*Little Me*
172	Reflection	*Mulan*
175	Sing	*Sesame Street*
178	So This Is Love (The Cinderella Waltz)	*Cinderella*
188	Someone's Waiting for You	*The Rescuers*
192	Tomorrow	*Annie*
181	The Ugly Duckling	*Hans Christian Andersen*
196	We're All in This Together	*High School Musical*
204	When I See an Elephant Fly	*Dumbo*
201	When You Wish upon a Star	*Pinocchio*
210	Where Is Love?	*Oliver!*
212	Who Will Buy?	*Oliver!*
216	With a Smile and a Song	*Snow White and the Seven Dwarfs*
218	The Work Song	*Cinderella*
224	Wouldn't It Be Loverly	*My Fair Lady*
207	You're Never Fully Dressed without a Smile	*Annie*
228	You've Got a Friend in Me	*Toy Story*
221	Zip-A-Dee-Doo-Dah	*Song of the South*

ANY DREAM WILL DO
from *Joseph and the Amazing Technicolor® Dreamcoat*

Music by Andrew Lloyd Webber
Lyrics by Tim Rice

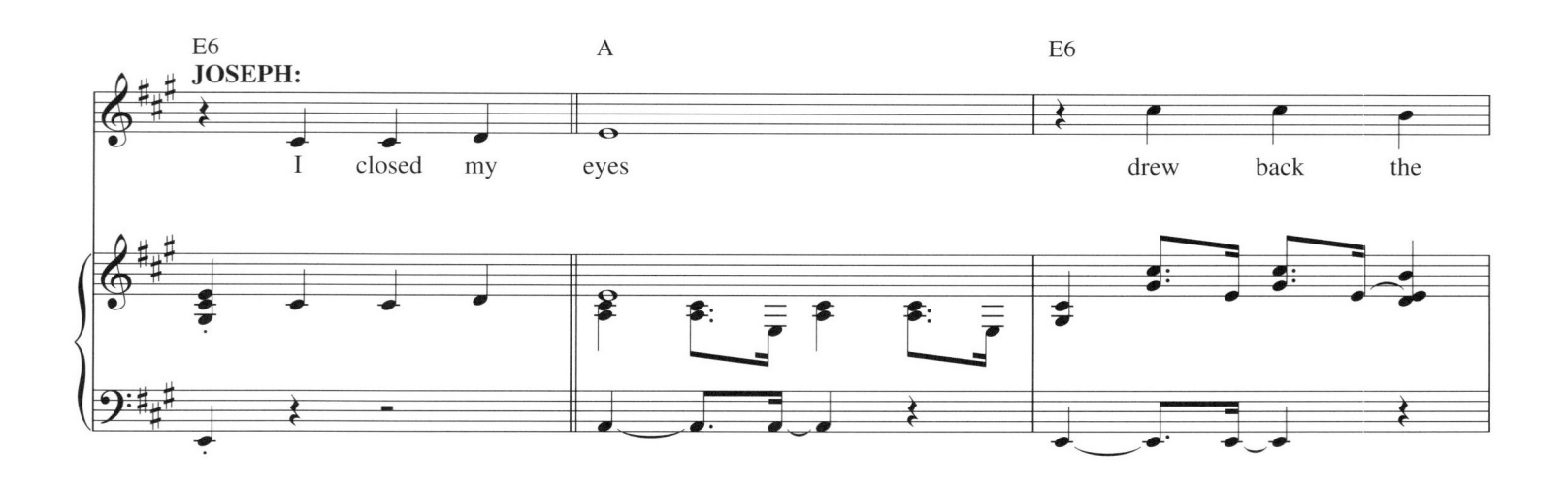

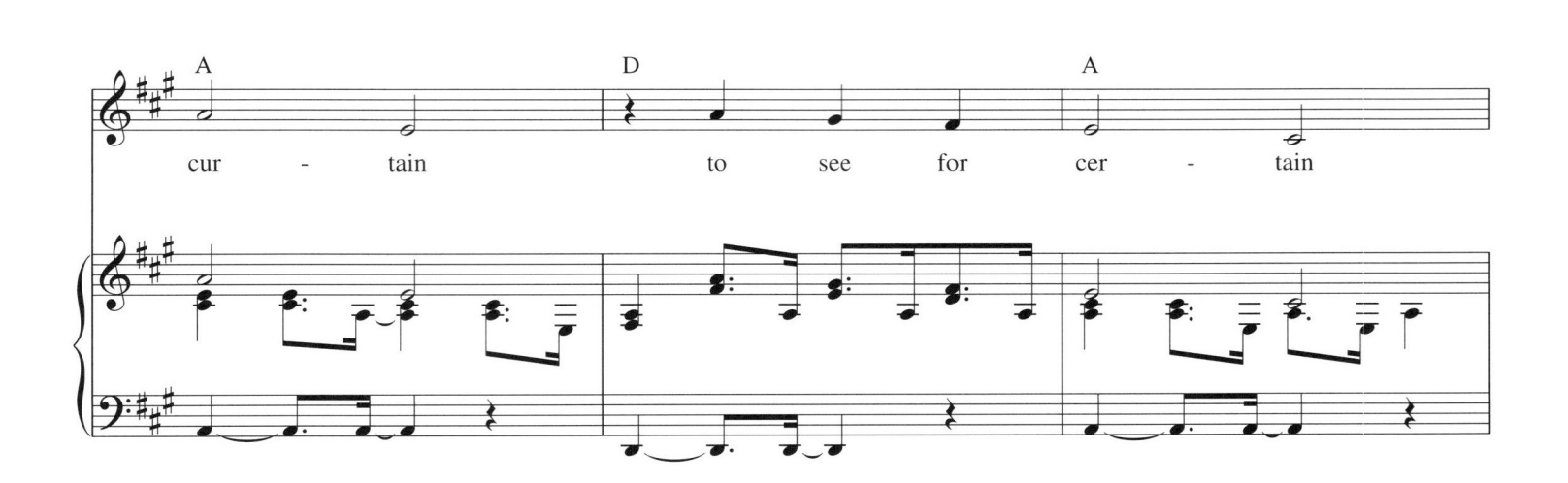

JOSEPH: I closed my eyes, drew back the cur-tain to see for cer-tain

© Copyright 1969 The Really Useful Group Ltd.
Copyright Renewed
International Copyright Secured   All Rights Reserved

what I thought I knew. Far far a-way someone was weep-ing, but the world was sleep-ing, an-y dream will do. I wore my coat with gold-en lin-ing, bright col-ours shin-ing won-der-ful and new.

And in the east the dawn was break-ing, and the world was wak-ing,

E7 A G/A A7
an - y dream will do.
A
D D6 Dmaj7 D6 B7 B
crash of drums a flash of light, my gold - en coat flew
B9 A/E E A E7 A/E E7 A/E
out of sight. The col - ours fad - ed in - to dark - ness,
E Bm/E E B7/E E Bm7/E
I was left a - lone.

E7 A E6
May I re - turn, to the be -
A D A
gin - ning, the light is dim - ming
E7 A E6 E7
and the dream is too, the world and
A E6 A
I, we are still wait - ing,

D
A
E
still hes - i - tat - ing
an - y dream will
A
Bm7/A
A
do,
Bm7/A
A
Bm7/A
an - y dream will
do,
A
Bm/E
A
rall.
an - y dream will
do.
rall.

BABY MINE
from Walt Disney's *Dumbo*

Words by Ned Washington
Music by Frank Churchill

Moderately slow

Ba - by mine _____ don't you cry. _____

Ba - by mine _____ dry your eye. _____

Rest your head close to my heart, nev - er to part, ba - by of

Copyright © 1941 by Walt Disney Productions
Copyright Renewed
World Rights Controlled by Bourne Co. (ASCAP)
International Copyright Secured   All Rights Reserved

C/E Dm7 C G9sus C G/B Am Am/G
3
mine. Lit - tle one when you
3
F6 Fm6 Fm6/G G7 C G/B Am Am/G
3
play don't you mind what they
3
F6 Fm6 Fm6/G G7 F F/E Dm7 Dm7/C
3
say. Let those eyes spar - kle and
3
F6 Fdim C/E Dm7 C E7
3 3
shine, nev - er a tear, ba - by of mine.
3 3

Somewhat faster

| Am | | Bm7 | E7sus | E7 |

If they knew sweet lit-tle you, _____

| Am | | Bm7 | E7sus | E7 |

they'd end up lov-ing you too. _____

| Am | Am/C | Em | Em/G | Am | Am/G |

All those same peo-ple who scold you, what they'd

| F♯m7♭5 | B7 | Em | B/D♯ | Dm7 | G7 | C | G/B |

give just for the right to hold you. From your

Am Am/G F6 Fm6 Fm6/G G7 C G/B
head to your toes, you're not
Am Am/G F6 Fm6 Fm6/G G7 F F/E
much, good-ness knows, but you're
Dm7 F6 Fdim G7♭9 C
so pre-cious to me, cute as can be, ba-by of mine.
F6 C F6 C

BE KIND TO YOUR PARENTS

from *Fanny*

Words and Music by
Harold Rome

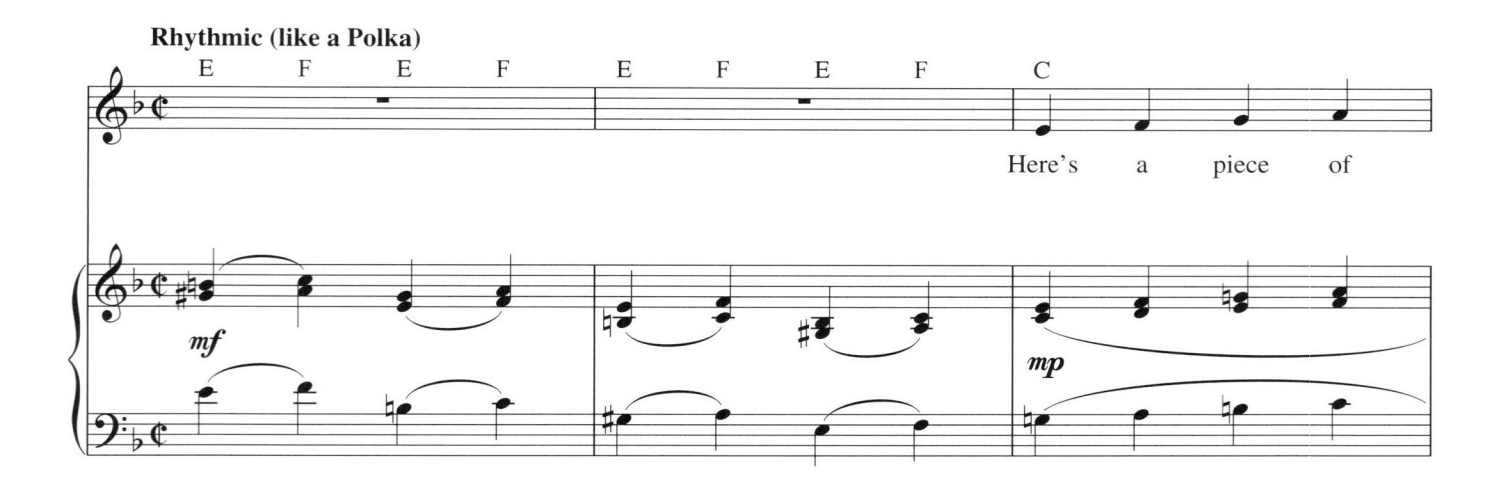

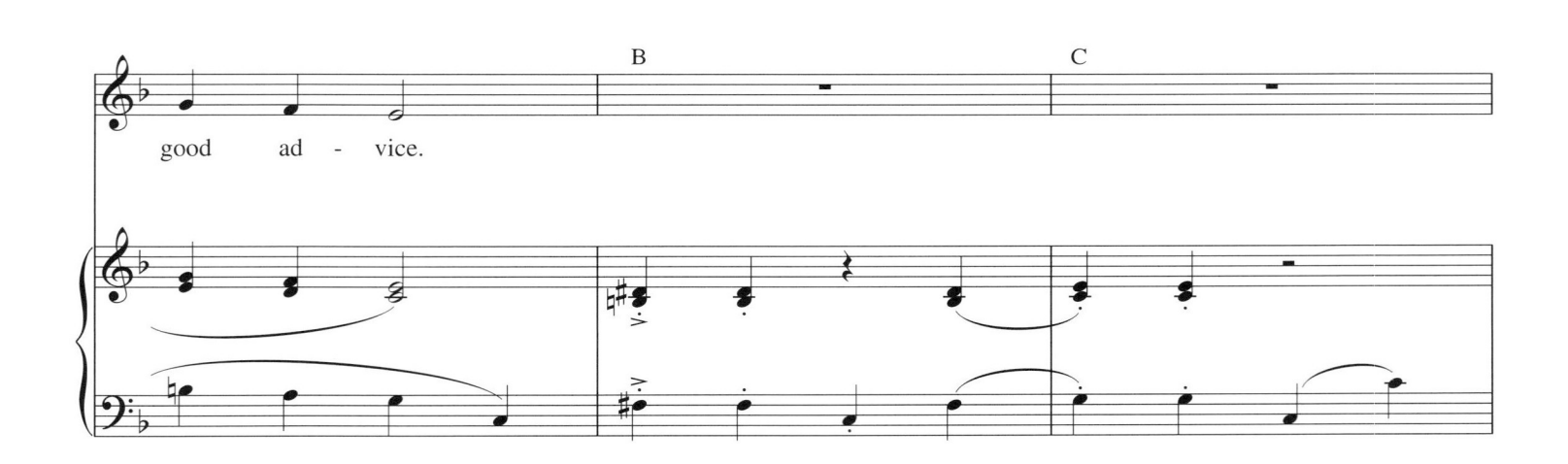

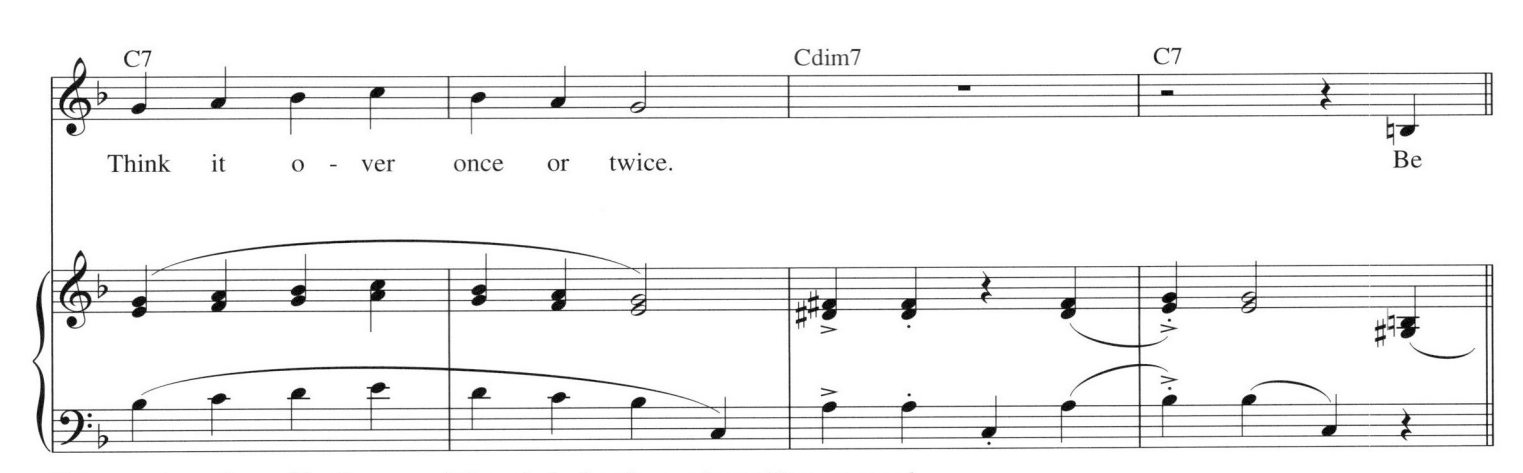

Rhythmic (like a Polka)

Here's a piece of good ad-vice. Think it o-ver once or twice. Be

This song is performed by Fanny and Cesario in the show, adapted here as a solo.

© 1954 (Renewed) CHAPPELL & CO., INC.
All Rights Reserved   Used by Permission

kind to your par - ents, though they don't de-

serve it. Re - mem - ber they're grown-ups, a

dif - fi - cult stage of life. They're apt to be

ner - vous, and o - ver - ex - cit - ed, con -

16

fused from their dai - ly storm and strife. Just keep in mind, though it sounds odd, I know, most par - ents once were chil - dren long a - go. In - cred - i - ble! So treat them with pa - tience and sweet un-der-stand-ing, in spite of the fool-ish things they do! Some-day you may wake up and find you're a par-ent, too. Be too.

BEIN' GREEN
from the Television Series *Sesame Street*

Words and Music by
Joe Raposo

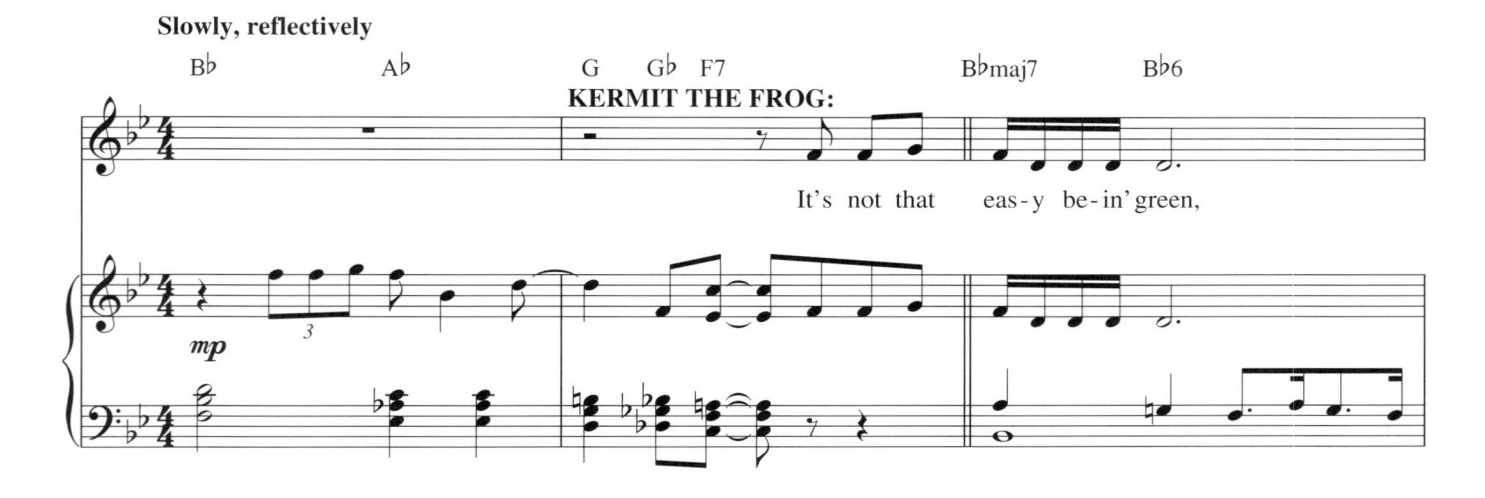

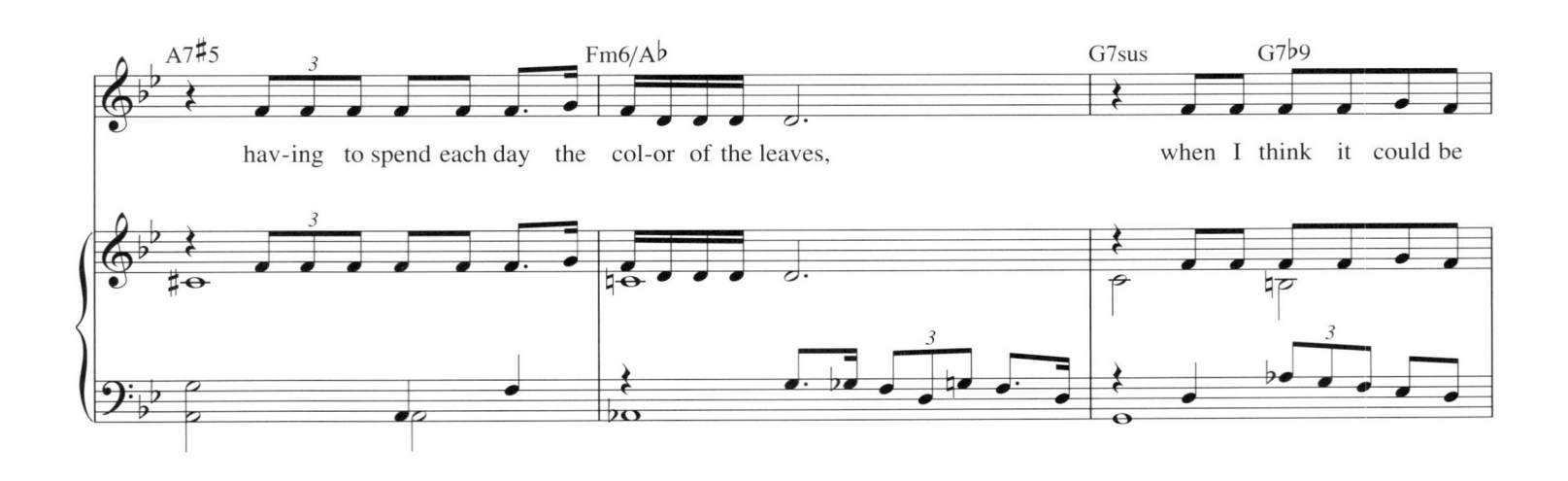

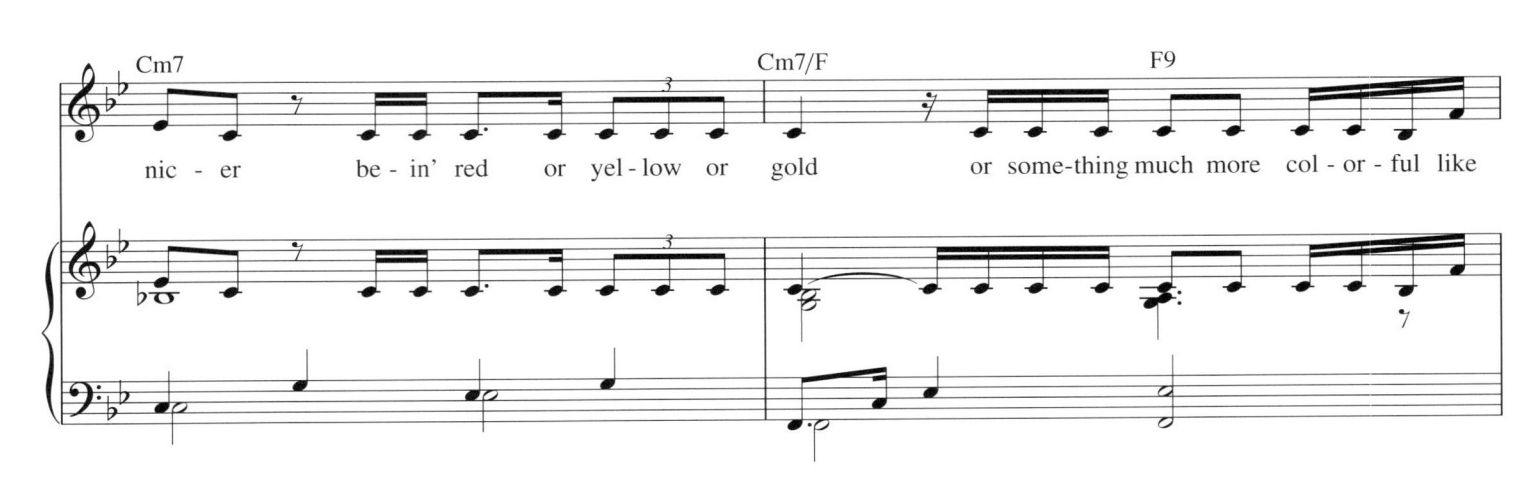

that. It's not eas-y be-in' green.

It seems you blend in with so man-y oth-er or-di-nar-y things, and peo-ple tend to pass you o-ver 'cause you're not stand-ing out like flash-y spar-kles on the wa-ter or stars in the sky.

Dm/A
A♭maj7
But green is the col - or of spring,
cresc.
mf
D♭maj7
B♭
Dm/A
and green can be cool and friend-ly - like,
and green can be
Gm7
Gm(maj7)
Gm7/C
C9
big like an o - cean or im - por - tant like a moun - tain or
cresc.
f
Cm7
Cm7/F
F7
tall like a tree.
When green is
decresc.
mp

all there is to be, it could make you wonder why, but why wonder, why wonder? I am green, and it-'ll do fine. It's beau-ti-ful, and I think it's what I want to be.

BORN TO ENTERTAIN
from *Ruthless*

Lyric by Joel Paley
Music by Marvin Laird

Moderate Swing

Some girls like to cook and sew; When I cook it's in a show. I was born to en-ter-tain. *spoken to audience: "How ya doin'?"* Some girls pre-fer to

Copyright © 1992 by NOHNERS MUSIC (ASCAP)
All Rights Reserved   Used by Permission

help mom clean, _ I'd rath - er learn a dance rou - tine. _

I _ was born to en - ter - tain. _

spoken to audience: "Where ya from?" In - stead of walk - in' I _ go f'- lap - pin',

When I tap, I make it hap - pen. _ Mom says I have

Broad-way on the brain.

Don't get too com-fy in that seat, When I strut my stuff you'll be on your feet. I was born to sing and dance.

Not ev-'ry show biz

*Pocatello (pronounced Pocatella) is a town in Idaho.

Edim7 Db/Ab Fm7b5 Cmaj7/F Db6/F Bb7#5
born to a - muse, From the tip of my nose to the tap of my shoes. So
Ebm9 Edim7 Db(add2)/F Db6 C7 Fdim7 Fm9b5
strike up the band, And hand me my hat and my cane,
Cb/Bb Bb9 D7#5 Ebm9 Edim7 Db(add2)/F Gbmaj7 G13#11 Ebm/Ab
'Cause I was born to en - ter -
Db7(#9) Db7/F Gb9 Gdim7 Db Cb Ab G Gb E C Db
tain.
gliss.

CASTLE ON A CLOUD
from *Les Misérables*

Music by Claude-Michel Schönberg
Lyrics by Alain Boublil, Jean-Marc Natel
and Herbert Kretzmer

COSETTE:
There is a cas - tle on a cloud.
There is a room that's full of toys.

I like to go there in my sleep.
There are a hun - dred boys and girls.

Music and Lyrics Copyright © 1980 by Editions Musicales Alain Boublil
English Lyrics Copyright © 1986 by Alain Boublil Music Ltd. (ASCAP)
Mechanical and Publication Rights for the U.S.A. Administered by Alain Boublil Music Ltd. (ASCAP) c/o Joel Faden & Co., Inc.,
1775 Broadway, Suite 708, New York, NY 10019, Tel. (212) 246-7203, Fax (212) 246-7217
International Copyright Secured. All Rights Reserved. This music is copyright. Photocopying is illegal.
All Performance Rights Restricted.

Aren't any floors for me to sweep,
Nobody shouts or talks too loud,

not in my castle on a cloud.
not in my castle on a cloud. There is a lady all in white, holds me and sings a lullaby. She's nice to see and she's soft to touch. She

says, "Co-sette, I love you ver-y much." I know a place where no one's lost. I know a place where no one cries. Cry-ing at all is not al-lowed, not in my cas-tle on a cloud.

THE CANDY MAN
from *Willy Wonka And The Chocolate Factory*

Words and Music by Leslie Bricusse
and Anthony Newley

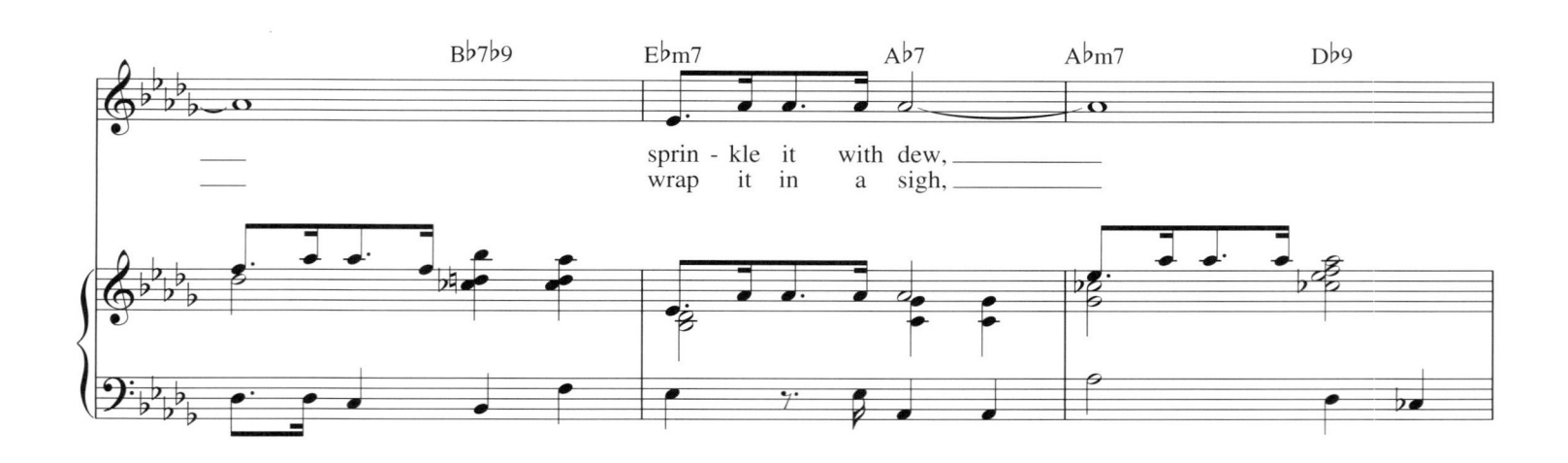

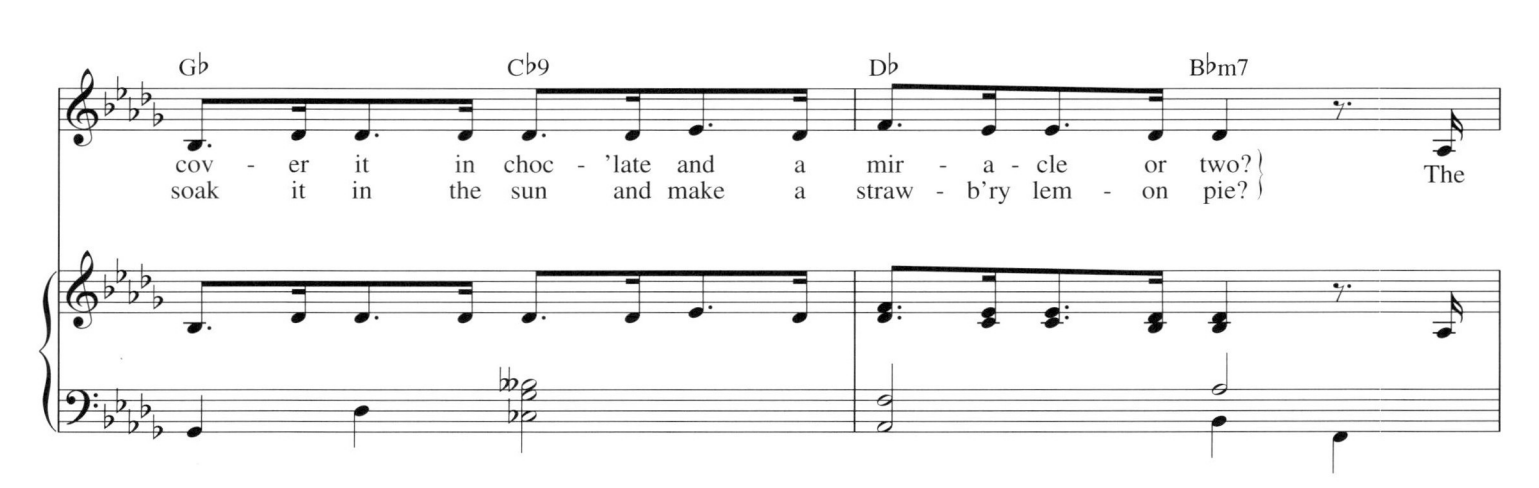

BILL:
Who can take a sunrise, sprinkle it with dew, cover it in choc-'late and a miracle or two?
Who can take a rainbow, wrap it in a sigh, soak it in the sun and make a straw-b'ry lemon pie?

The

Copyright © 1970, 1971 by Taradam Music, Inc.
Copyright Renewed
International Copyright Secured All Rights Reserved

candy man, the candy man can, the candy man can 'cause he mixes it with love and makes the world taste good. The candy man makes ev-'ry-thing he bakes sat-is-fy-ing and deli - cious. Talk a - bout your child - hood wish - es! You can e - ven eat the dish - es! Who can take to - mor - row, ____ dip it in a dream, ____ sep - a - rate the sor - row and col - lect up all the cream? The can - dy man, ____

the can-dy man can, the can-dy man can 'cause he mix-es it with love and makes the world taste good. The And the world tastes good 'cause the can-dy man thinks it should.

CONSIDER YOURSELF
from the Broadway Musical *Oliver!*

Words and Music by
Lionel Bart

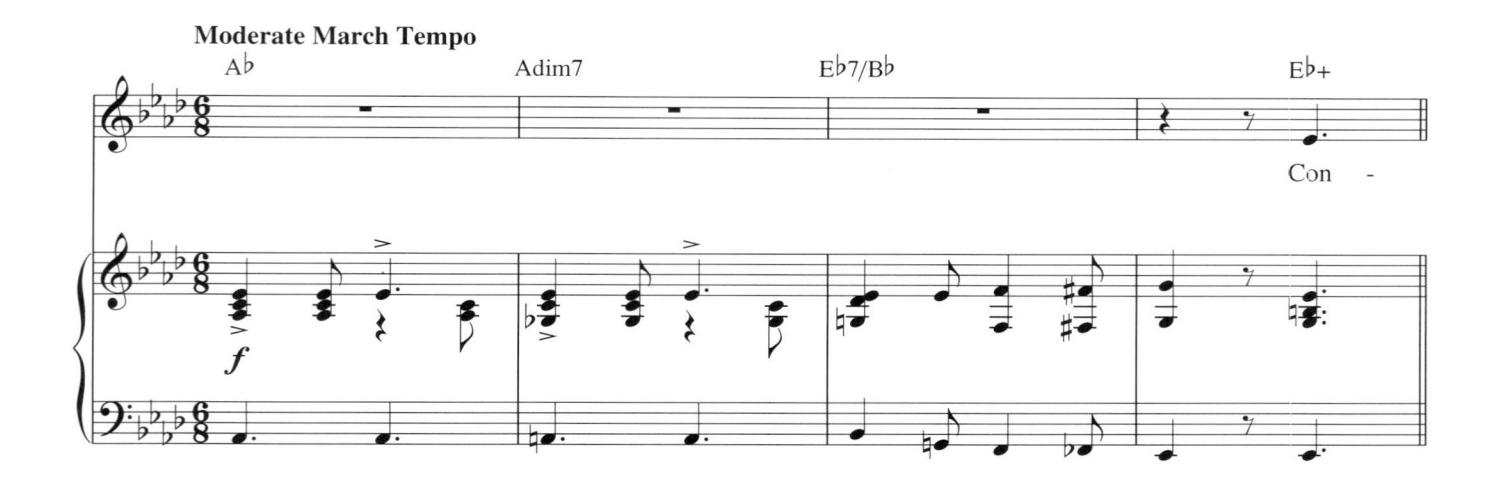

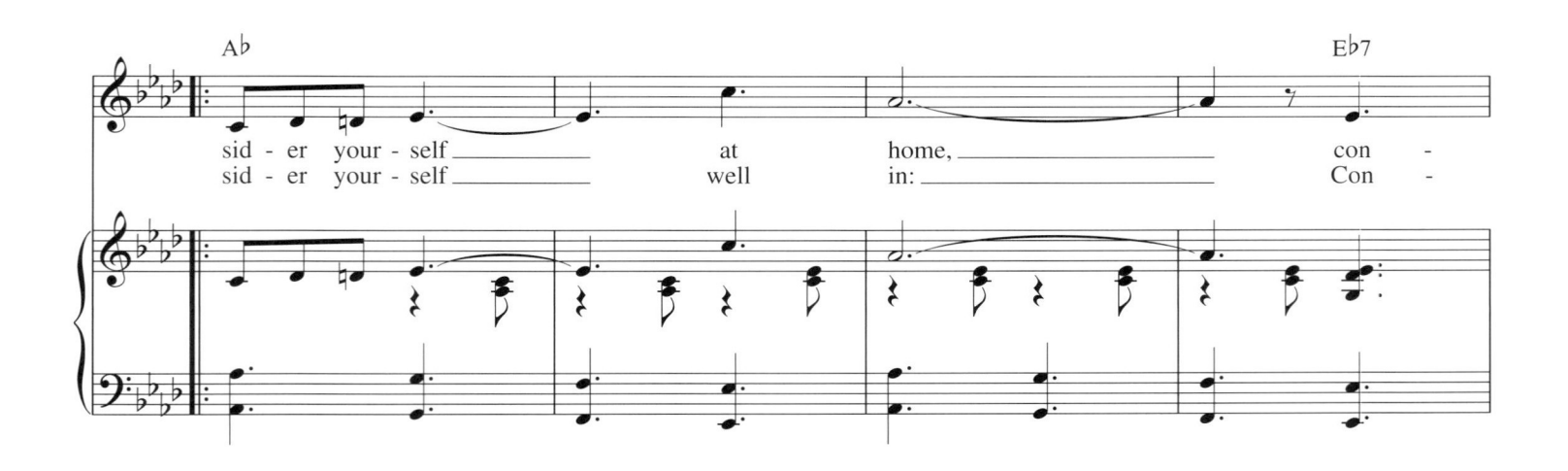

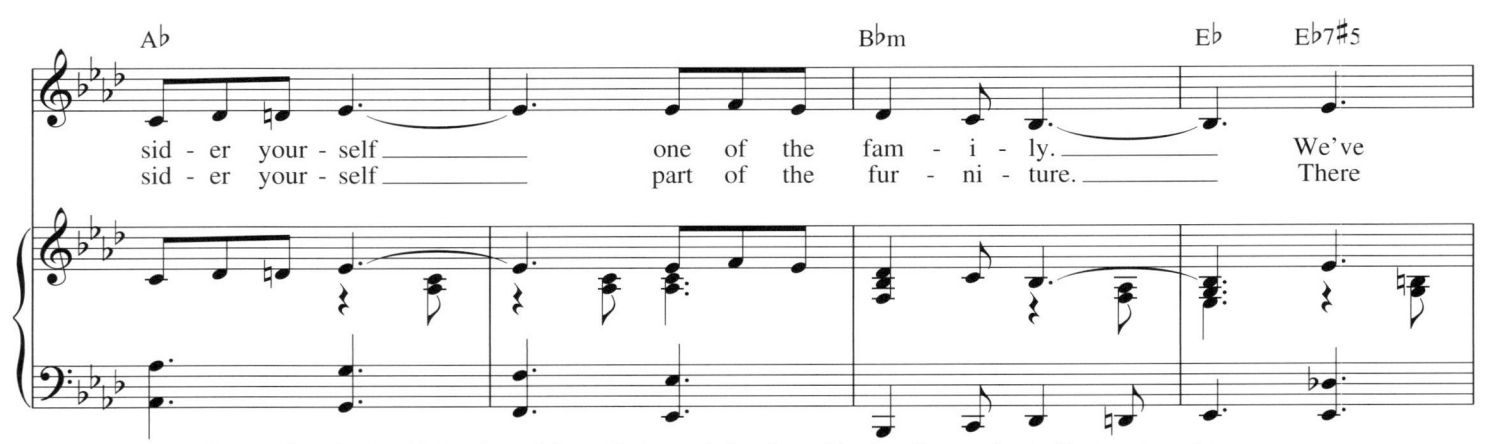

Moderate March Tempo

Con-sider yourself at home, consider yourself one of the family. We've
Con-sider yourself well in: Consider yourself part of the furniture. There

This song is performed by The Artful Dodger, Oliver Twist and the Crowd in the show, adapted here as a solo.

tak-en to you ____ so strong, _____ it's
is-n't a lot ____ to spare; _____ who

clear we're go-ing to get a-long! Con-
cares? What-ev-er we've got we

share! If it should chance to be we should see some hard-er days, ____
tries to be lah-di-dah and up-pit-y, ____

___ emp-ty lard-er days, _____ why grouse? _____
___ there's a cup o' tea _____ for all. _____

Al - ways a chance we'll meet some - bod - y to foot the bill,
On - ly it's wise to be han - dy wiv a roll - ing pin

then the drinks are on the house!
when the land - lord comes to call!

Con - sid - er your - self our mate,

we don't want to have no fuss.

E♭7 E♭7♯5 A♭ Cm7♭5
For aft - er some con - sid - er - a - tion, we can
F7 B♭m D♭m/F♭
state: Con - sid - er your - self
1
E♭7
one of
A♭7
us. No - bod - y
2
E♭7 E♭13
one of
A♭
us.
ff

CRUELLA DE VIL
from Walt Disney's *101 Dalmatians*

Words and Music by
Mel Leven

Slow Blues

ROGER: Cru-ella de Vil, Cru-ella de Vil, if she doesn't scare you, no e-vil thing will. To see her is to take a sud-den chill. Cru-ella, Cru-ella de Vil. The curl of her lips, the

© 1959 Walt Disney Music Company
Copyright Renewed
All Rights Reserved   Used by Permission

ice in her stare; all in-no-cent chil-dren had bet-ter be-ware. She's like a spi-der wait-ing for the kill. Look out for Cru-el-la de Vil. At first you think Cru-el-la is the dev-il, But af-ter time has worn a-way the shock, you come to re-a-lize you've seen her kind of eyes watching you from underneath a rock. This vampire bat, this inhuman beast, she ought to be locked up and never released. The world was such a wholesome place until Cruella, Cruella de Vil.

EV'RYBODY WANTS TO BE A CAT
from Walt Disney's *The Aristocats*

Words by Floyd Huddleston
Music by Al Rinker

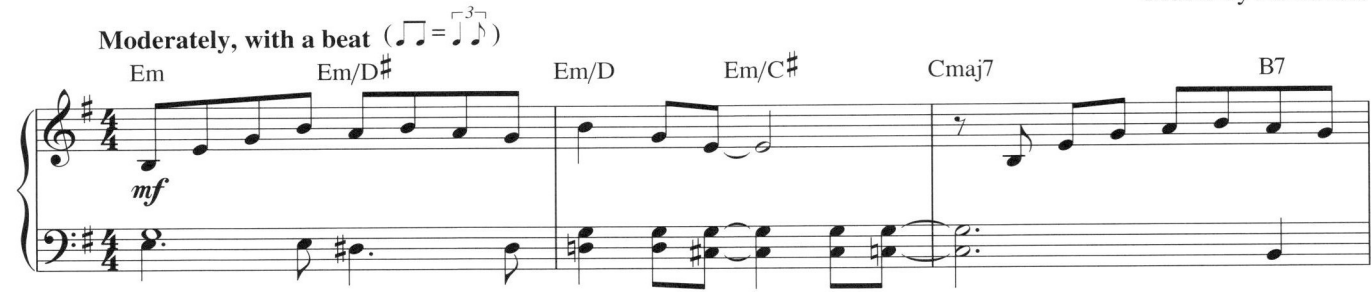

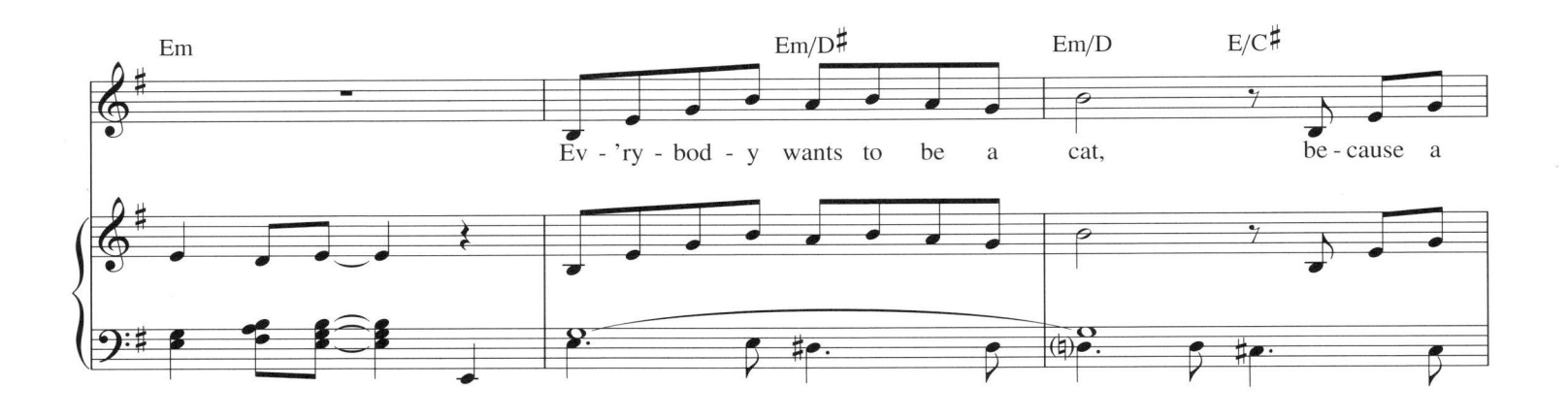

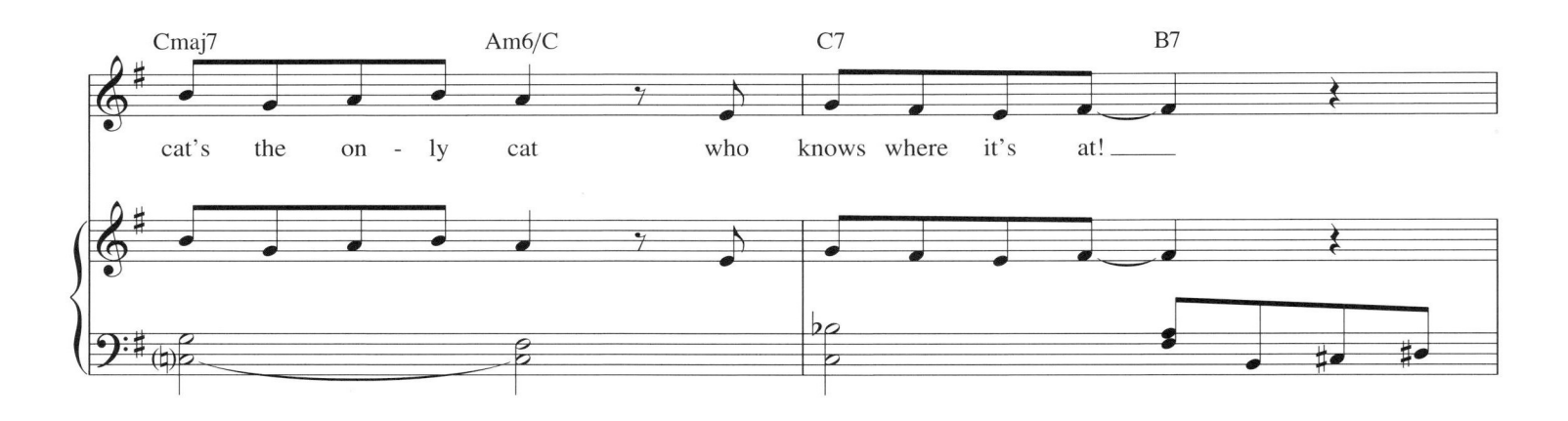

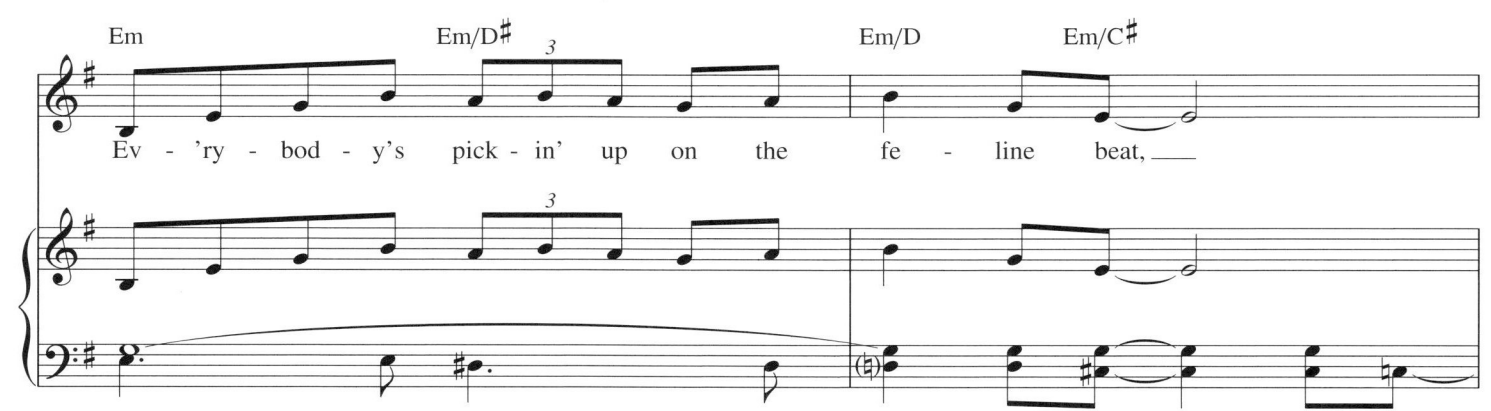

This song is performed by The Cats in the film, adapted here as a solo.

© 1968 Walt Disney Music Company
Copyright Renewed
All Rights Reserved   Used by Permission

'cause ev-'ry-thing else is ob-so-lete. Be-ware of a square when he of-fers to share his milk to sip! If it has-n't been tried, I sug-gest you pro-vide your own cat-nip. I've heard some corn-y birds who tried to sing. But still a cat's the on-ly cat who knows how to swing! A purr be-tween two fur-ry friends may be old hat, But ev-'ry-bod-y wants to be a cat! Be be a cat!

DREAM FOR YOUR INSPIRATION
from *The Muppets Take Manhattan*

Words and Music by
Scott Brownlee

I used to think that I was just a no count.
I used to think that I would get no-where. But then I learned that when I'm feel-in' low down, I'm back up on my feet if I re-mem-ber all my dreams.

© 1984 Fuzzy Muppet Songs
All Rights Reserved   Used by Permission

I used to get to feeling so down hearted, I used to e-ven hate the
I used to think that I was nothing special, that I was just an-oth-er
So if you think that you are me-di-o-cre, and ev-'ry-thing you do is

col-or green. But ev-'ry time I think I can't get start-ed, I
pret-ty face. But now I know that I will be suc-cess-ful
just so-so, And if you're wish-in' you could start all o-ver,

think of all my dreams and then I'm right back on the beam. You've got to dream for your
if I al-ways do just what I real-ly want to do. You've got to dream of your
stop and re-al-ize you've got your dreams and you'll be fine. You've got to

in-spir-a-tion. Dream of what you can do, 'cause with your
se-cret wish-es. Dream of your high-est hopes, 'cause if you

dreams and some per-spir-a-tion, an-y-thing with-in your dream-ing is with-in your reach.
dream, you can

make your dreams come true._____ When you've

fin-'lly de-cid-ed things aren't as bad as they seem,__

You just can't de-ny__ it, where there's a will there's a dream. Yeah! You've got to

G G/B C G G/B D
dream for your in - spir - a - tion. Dream of what you can do, 'cause if you
G G/B C D7
dream, you can make your dreams come true. You've got to
G D7 G D7 G D.S. al Coda
dream, dream.
CODA
G G/B
dream for your
C G G/B D
in - spir - a - tion. Dream of what you can do, 'cause with your

dreams and some per-spir-a-tion, an-y-thing with-in your dream-ing is with-in your reach. You've got to dream of your se-cret wish-es. Dream of your high-est hopes, 'cause if you dream, you can make your dreams come true. You've got to dream.

FRIEND
from *Snoopy!!!*

Words by Hal Clayton Hackady
Music by Larry Grossman

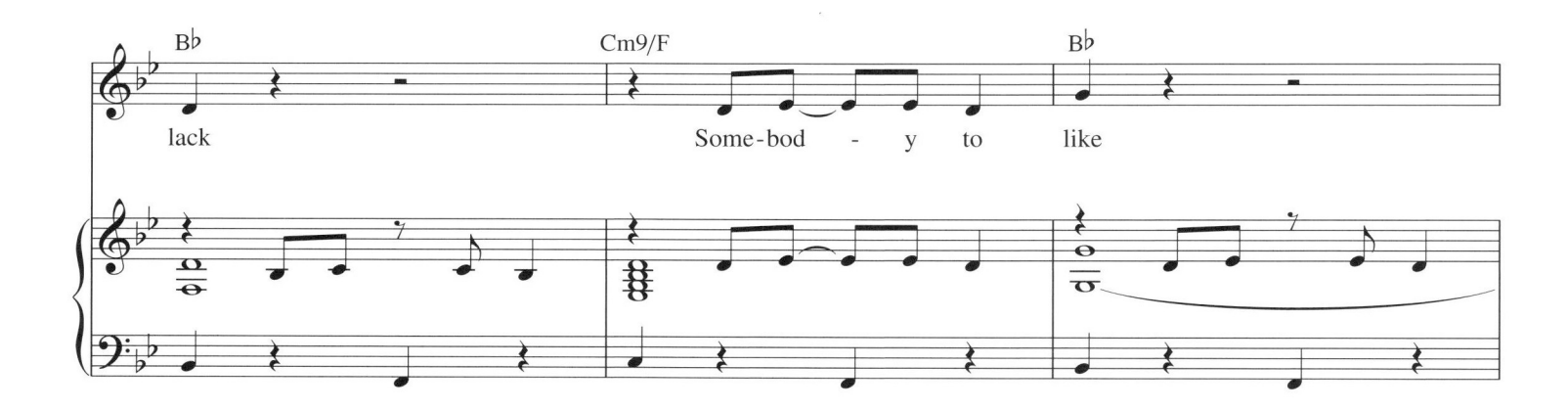

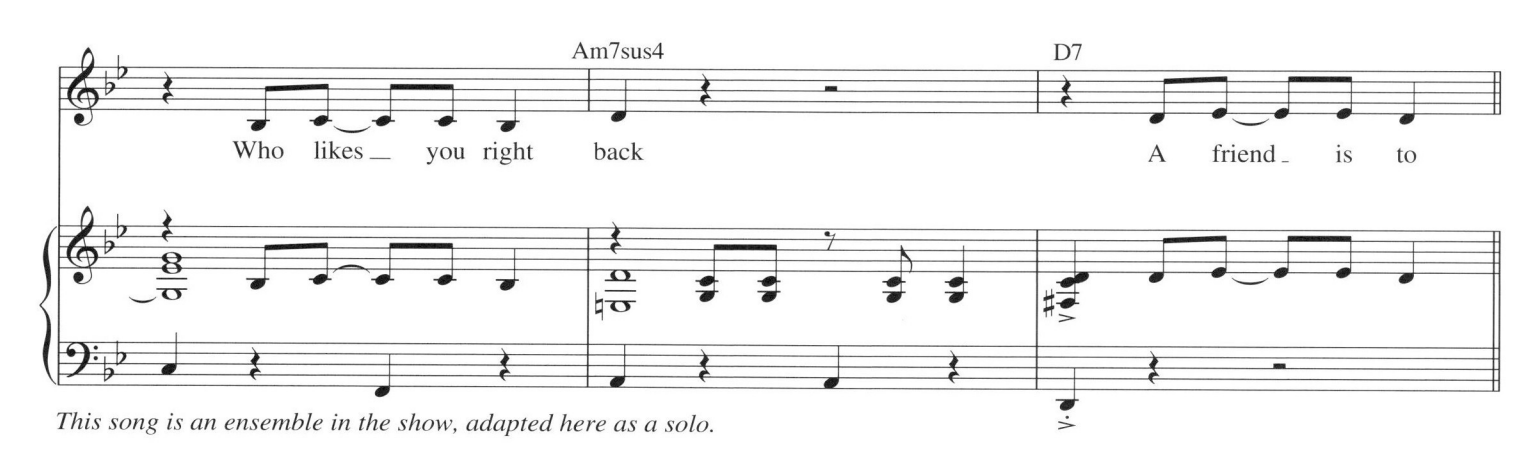

This song is an ensemble in the show, adapted here as a solo.

Copyright © 1976 by Unichappell Music Inc.
Copyright Renewed
International Copyright Secured   All Rights Reserved

please A friend is to cheer To help through the night, A friend is to write: "I wish you were here!" A friend is to trust and fight to defend. A friend is a must When you need a

Lyrics:

friend
You on-ly need one
And friend_ when you do
Your ver-y best friend, your friend_ to the end had bet-ter be you.
Had bet-ter be you.
A friend is to you!

FEED THE BIRDS
from Walt Disney's *Mary Poppins*

Words and Music by Richard M. Sherman
and Robert B. Sherman

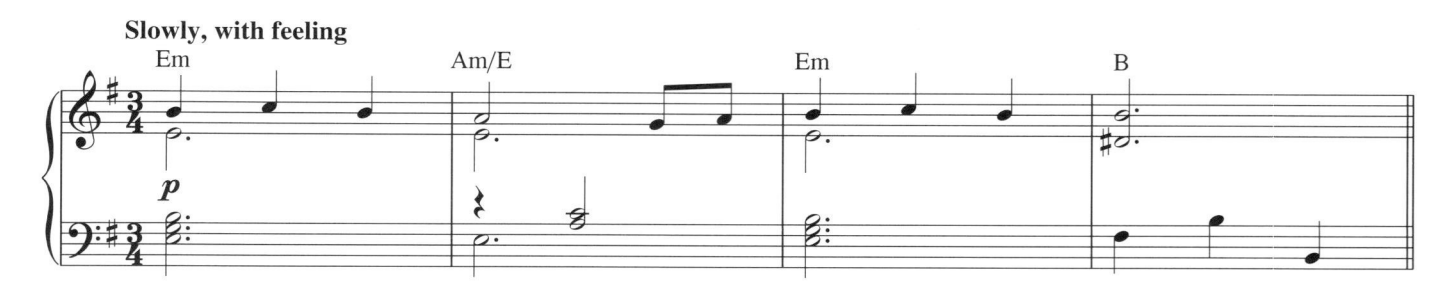

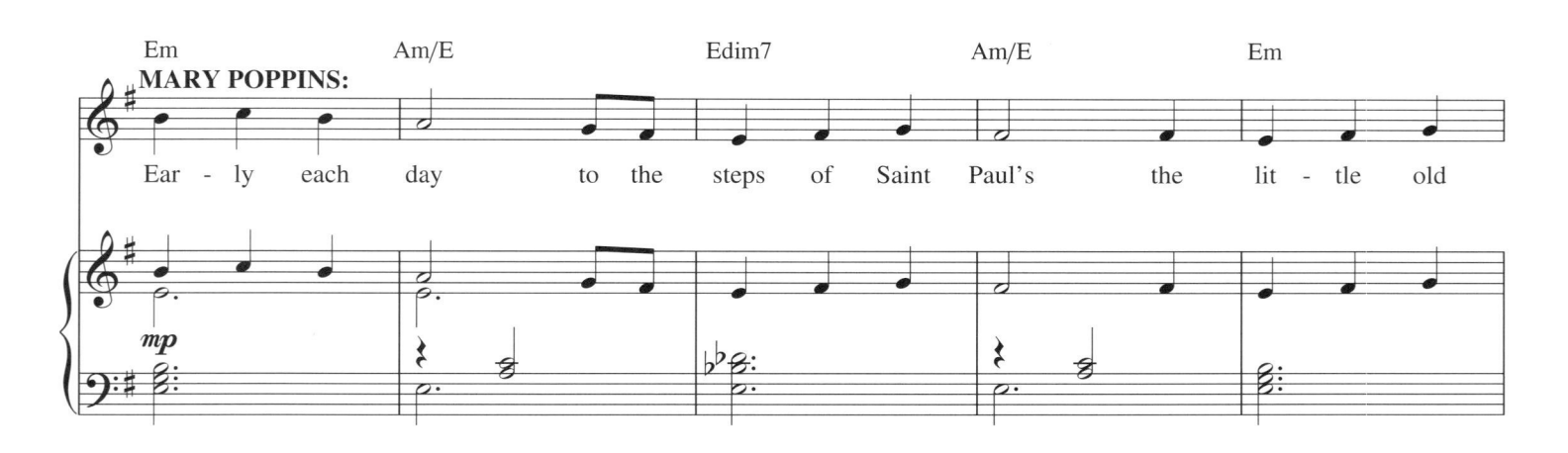

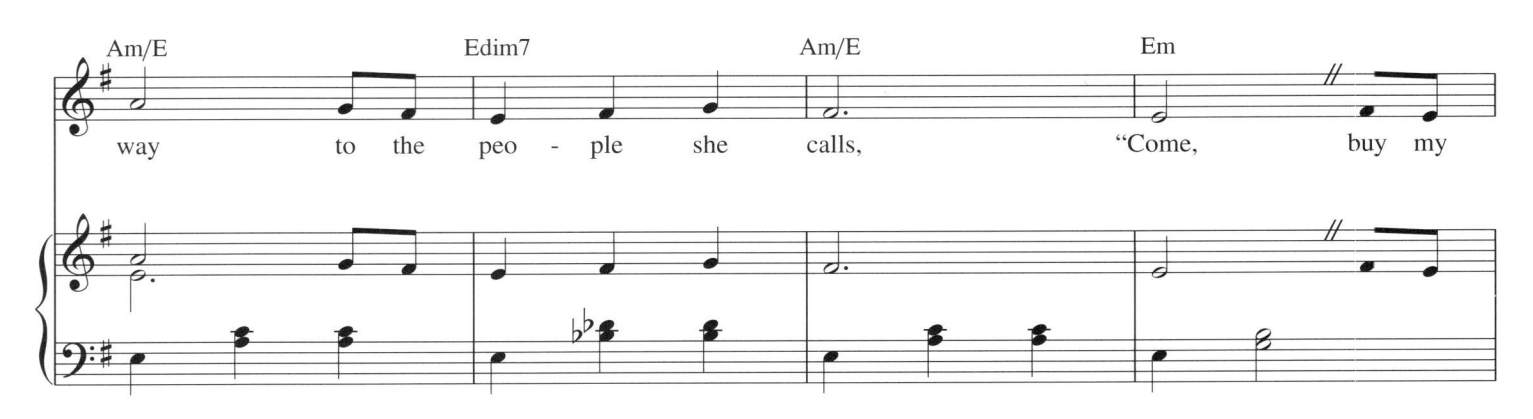

Slowly, with feeling

MARY POPPINS:
Early each day to the steps of Saint Paul's the little old bird wom-an comes. In her own spe-cial way to the peo-ple she calls, "Come, buy my

© 1963 Wonderland Music Company, Inc.
Copyright Renewed
All Rights Reserved   Used by Permission

bags full of crumbs. Come feed the little birds, show them you care, and you'll be glad if you do. Their young ones are hungry, their nests are so bare; all it takes is tuppence from

Em
D7
G
G/B
opt.
you.
Feed the birds,
rall.
mf a tempo
C
G
C
G
tup - pence a bag,
tup - pence,
tup - pence,
A7
D7
G
G/B
tup - pence a bag.
Feed the birds,"
(If only chorus is sung) the
C
G
C
G
D7
that's what she
bird wom - an
cries,
while o - ver - head,
her birds fill the

Slightly faster

skies. All a-round the ca-the-dral the saints and a-pos-tles look down as she sells her wares. Al-though you can't see it, you know they are smil-ing each time some-one shows that he cares.

rit.

Though her words are simple and few, listen, listen, she's calling to you: "Feed the birds, tuppence a bag, tuppence, tuppence, tuppence a bag."

GARY, INDIANA

from Meredith Willson's *The Music Man*

By Meredith Willson

© 1954, 1957, 1958, 1959 (Renewed) FRANK MUSIC CORP. and MEREDITH WILLSON MUSIC
All Rights Reserved

an - a, that's the town that knew me when. If you'd like to have a logical explanation how I happened on this elegant syncopation, I will say without a moment of hesitation, there is just one place that can light my face. Ga-ry, In-di-an-a, Ga-ry, In-di-an-a, not Lou-i-si-an-a, Par-is, France, New York or Rome, but Ga-ry, In-di-an-a, Ga-ry, In-di-an-a, Ga-ry, In-di-an-a, my home sweet home. If you'd home.

GETTING TO KNOW YOU
from *The King And I*

Lyrics by Oscar Hammerstein II
Music by Richard Rodgers

Moderato

It's a ver-y an-cient say-ing But a true and hon-est thought, That if you be-come a teach-er, by your pu-pils you'll be taught. As a teach-er, I've been

This song is an ensemble number in the show, adapted here as a solo.

Copyright © 1951 by Richard Rodgers and Oscar Hammerstein II
Copyright Renewed
Williamson Music, a Division of Rodgers & Hammerstein: an Imagem Company, owner of publication and allied rights throughout the world
International Copyright Secured   All Rights Reserved

| Edim7 | B♭/F | G9 | Gm7/C Gm7 |

learn - ing (You'll for - give me if I boast.) And I've now be - come an

| C9 | Cm7/F | *(Spoken)* | F7 |

ex - pert On the sub - ject I like most, Get - ting to know you.

Refrain *(gracefully and not fast)*
| B♭ | | Cm7(add4) F7 |

Get - ting to know you, get - ting to know all a - bout you

mp tranquillo

| Cm7(add4) F7 | Cm7 F7 | Cm7 F7 | B♭ |

Get - ting to like you, get - ting to hope you like me

Getting to know you, Putting it my way, but nicely

You are precisely My cup of tea!

Getting to know you, getting to feel free and easy

When I am with you, getting to know what to say.

Haven't you noticed? Suddenly I'm bright and breezy Because of all the beautiful and new things I'm learning about you day by day.

GOD HELP THE OUTCASTS
from Walt Disney's *The Hunchback of Notre Dame*

Music by Alan Menken
Lyrics by Stephen Schwartz

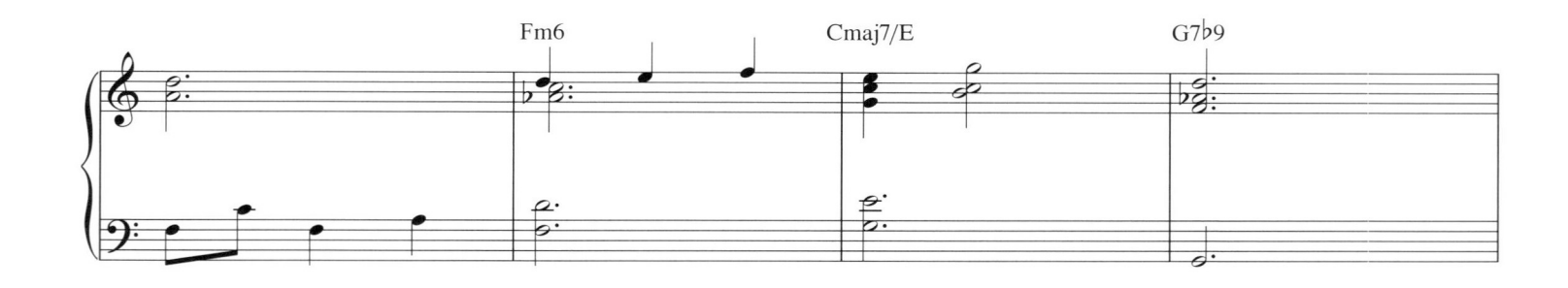

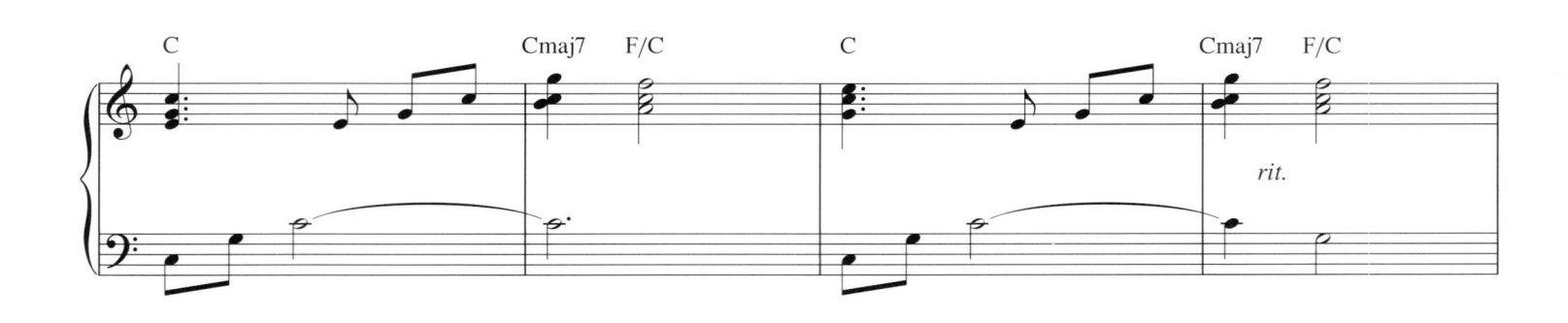

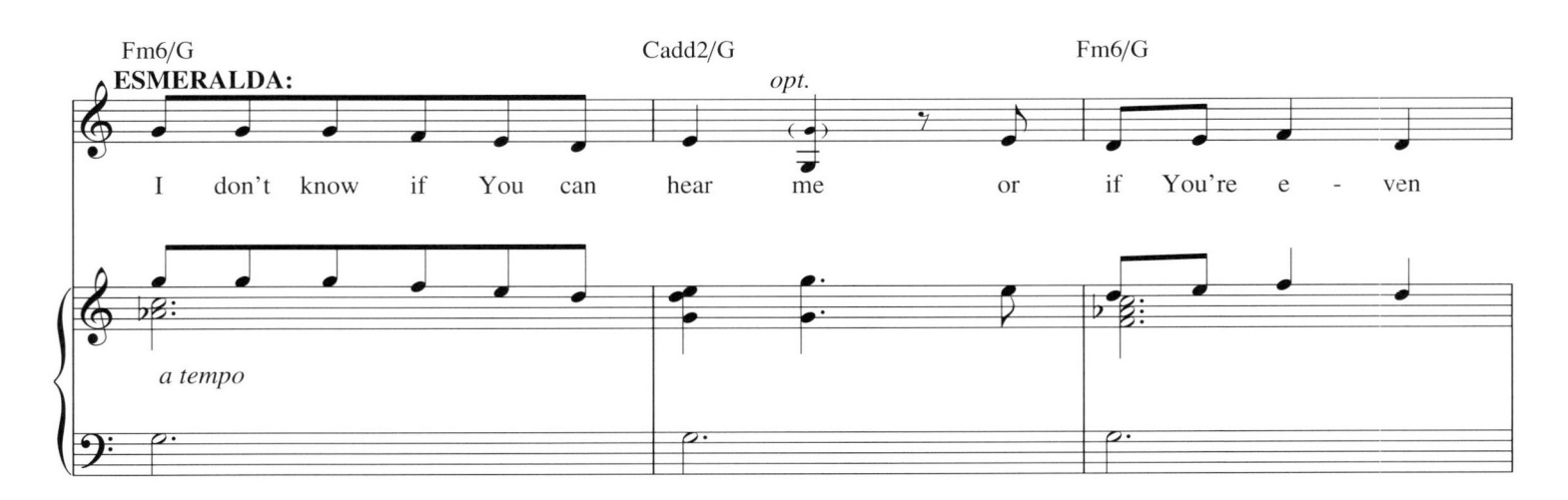

ESMERALDA: I don't know if You can hear me or if You're e-ven

© 1996 Wonderland Music Company, Inc. and Walt Disney Music Company
All Rights Reserved   Used by Permission

there, I don't know if You will listen to a humble prayer. They tell me I am just an outcast; I shouldn't speak to You. Still I see Your face and wonder: were You once an outcast, too?

God help the out-casts, hun-gry from birth.
I ask for noth-ing, I can get by.

Show them the mer-cy they don't find on earth.
But I know so man-y less luck-y than I.

The lost and
God help the

got - ten, they look to You still.
out - casts, the poor and down - trod.

God help the out - casts or no-bod - y
I thought we all were the chil - dren of

1.
will.

2.
God. I don't know if there's a rea - son why

some are blessed, some not. Why the few You seem to fa - vor, they fear us, flee us try not to see us. God help the outcasts, the tattered, the

torn, seek - ing an an - swer to why they were born. Winds of mis - for - tune have blown them a - bout. You made the out - casts; don't cast them out. The poor and un - luck - y, the weak and the odd; ____ I thought we all were the chil-dren of God. ____

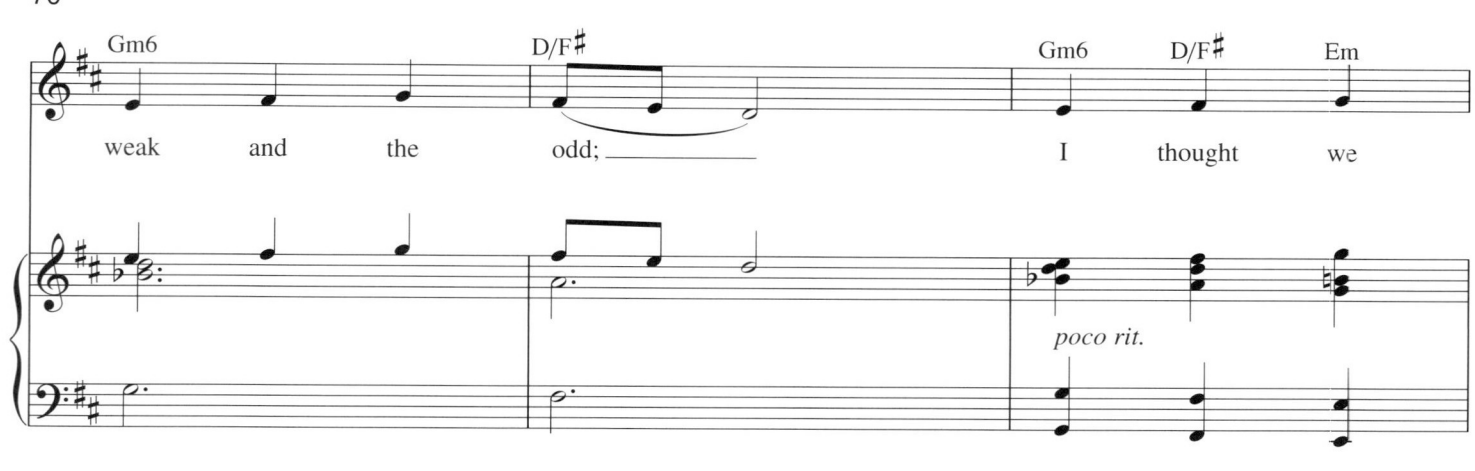

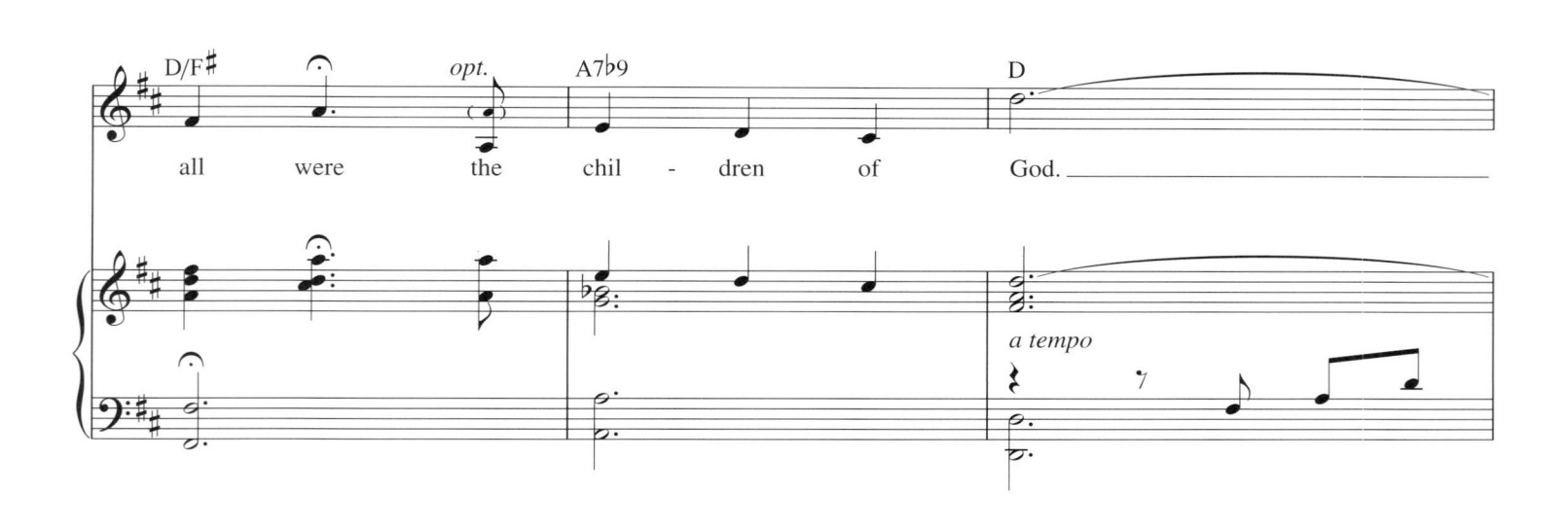

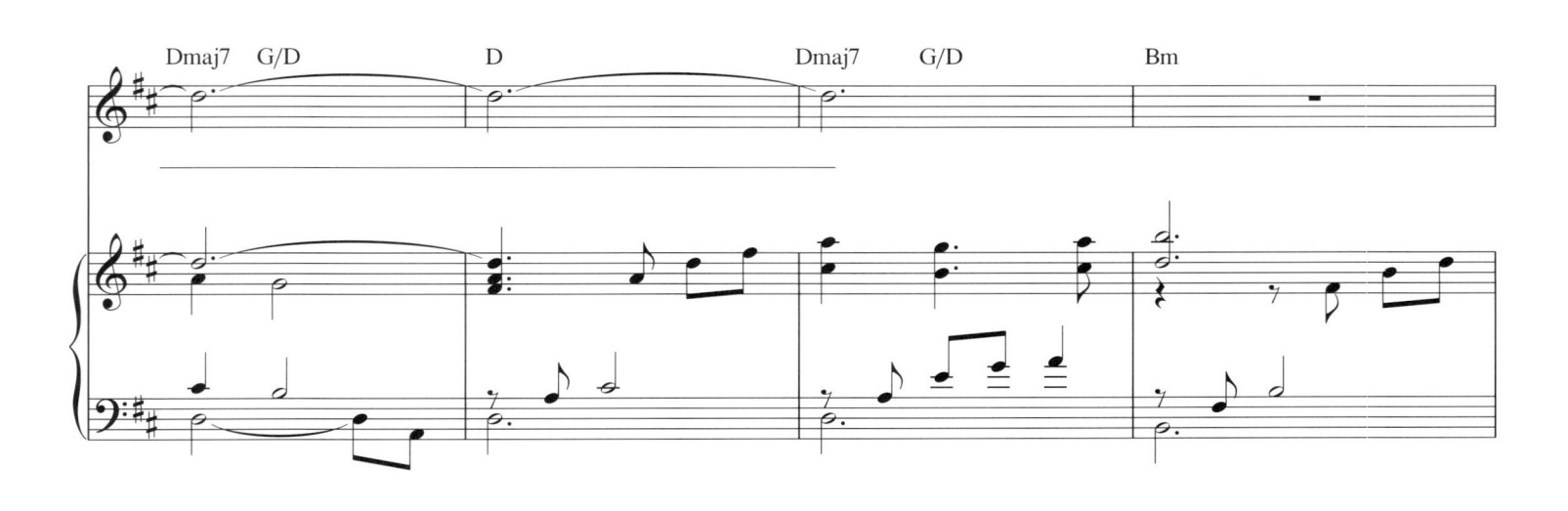

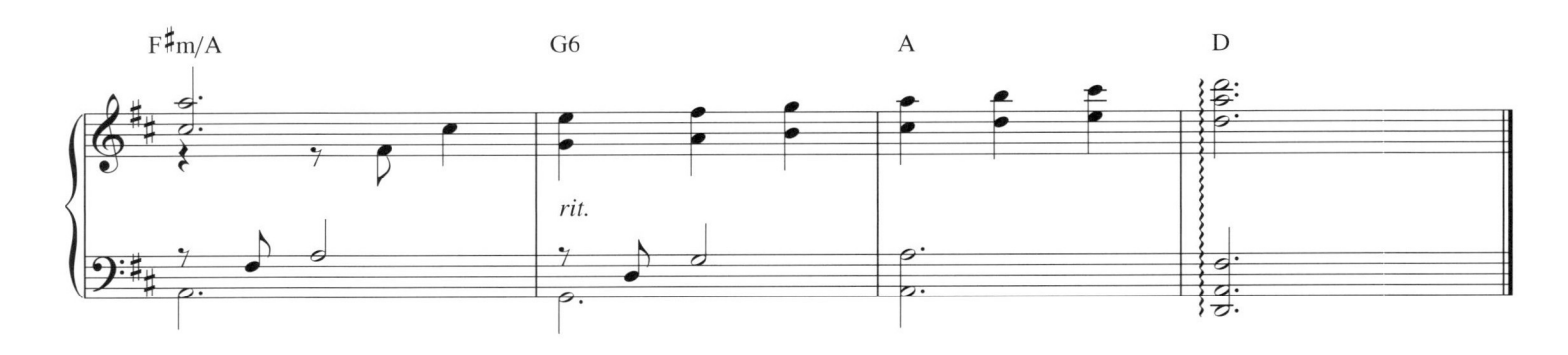

HAPPINESS
from *You're a Good Man, Charlie Brown*

Words and Music by
Clark Gesner

Broadly

Hap-pi-ness is two kinds of ice cream, find-ing your skate key, tell-ing the time. Hap-pi-ness is
Hap-pi-ness is five dif-f'rent cray-ons, know-ing a se-cret, climb-ing a tree. Hap-pi-ness is

This song is performed by the Company in the show, adapted here as a solo.

© 1965 JEREMY MUSIC INC.
© Renewed 1993 MPL MUSIC PUBLISHING, INC.
All Rights Reserved

learn - ing to whis - tle, ty - ing your shoe for the ver - y first time.
find - ing a nick - el, catch - ing a fire - fly, set - ting him free.

Hap - pi - ness is play - ing the drum in your
Hap - pi - ness is be - ing a - lone ev - 'ry

own school band. And hap - pi - ness is walk - ing hand in
now and then. And hap - pi - ness is com - ing home a -

hand.
gain.

Hap-pi-ness is morn-ing and eve-ning, day-time and night-time too. For hap-pi-ness is an-y-one, and an-y-thing at all, that's loved by you.

I ALWAYS KNEW
from *Annie Warbucks*

Lyric by Martin Charnin
Music by Charles Strouse
Arranged by Michael Dansicker

Moderato (in 2)

ANNIE:
I al-ways knew, knew that to-mor-row would come true____ I al-ways knew.____ When it was dark, with not one star up in the sky____ hey, I still knew.

© 1993 Charles Strouse
Worldwide publishing by Charles Strouse Publishing (Administered by Williamson Music, a division of Rodgers & Hammerstein: an Imagen Company)
All Rights Reserved   Used by Permission
www.CharlesStrouse.com

I said my prayers and I would go to sleep be-lieving___ I guess the trick is that you gotta keep be-lieving!___ 'Cause when you do, there go your tears, there goes_ your dark-

-est night, and the light breaks through I al-ways hoped, I al-ways dreamed, boy, how I hoped, boy how I dreamed, no that ain't true. I always knew I al-ways knew!

I DON'T NEED ANYTHING BUT YOU

from the Musical Production *Annie*

Lyric by Martin Charnin
Music by Charles Strouse

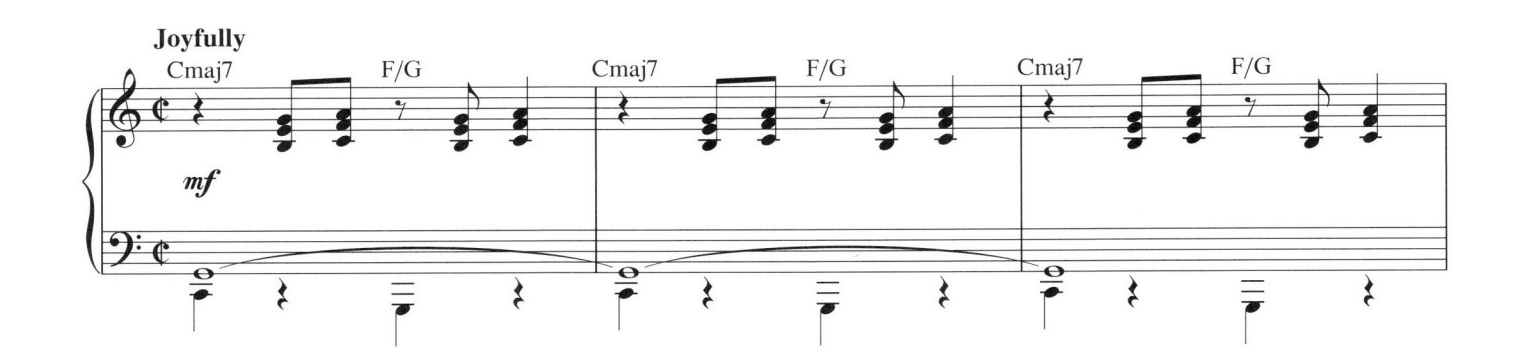

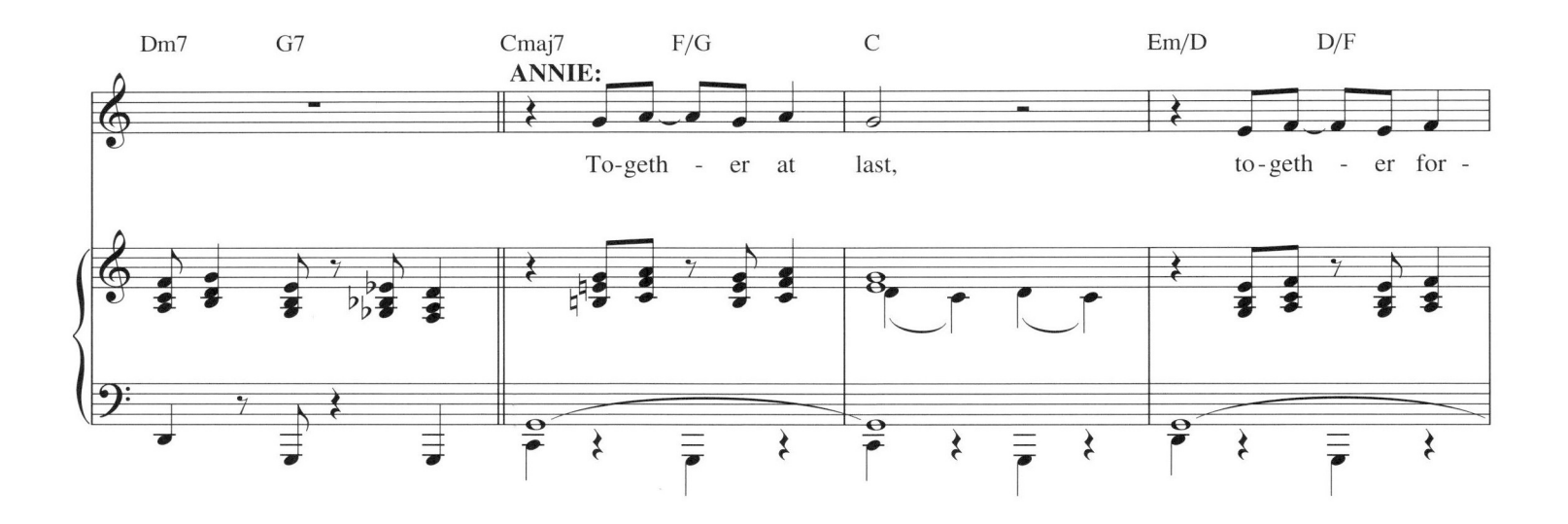

Joyfully

ANNIE:
To-geth-er at last, to-geth-er for-ev-er; we're ty-ing a knot they nev-er can

This song is performed by Oliver Warbucks and Annie in the show, adapted here as a solo for Annie.

© 1977 (Renewed) EDWIN H. MORRIS & COMPANY, A Division of MPL Music Publishing, Inc. and CHARLES STROUSE
All rights on behalf of CHARLES STROUSE owned by CHARLES STROUSE PUBLISHING (Administered by WILLIAMSON MUSIC,
a Division of Rodgers & Hammerstein: an Imagem Company)
All Rights Reserved   Used by Permission
www.CharlesStrouse.com

sev - er. I don't need sun-shine now to turn my skies to blue, I don't need an-y-thing but you! You wrapped me a-round your cute lit-tle fin-ger. You made life a

song you made me the singer. And what's that bath-tub tune I always "Bub-buh-boo?" I don't need an-y-thing but you! Yes-ter-day was plain aw-ful. You can say that again. Yes - ter - day __ was plain aw - ful, but that's not now, that's then. I'm poor __ as a mouse, You're rich - er than Mi - das! But noth - ing on earth could ev - er di -

vide us. And if to-mor-row I'm an ap-ple sell-er too. I don't need an-y-thing, an-y-thing, an-y-thing. I don't need an-y-thing but you!

I DON'T WANT TO LIVE ON THE MOON

from the Television Series *Sesame Street*

Words and Music by
Jeff Moss

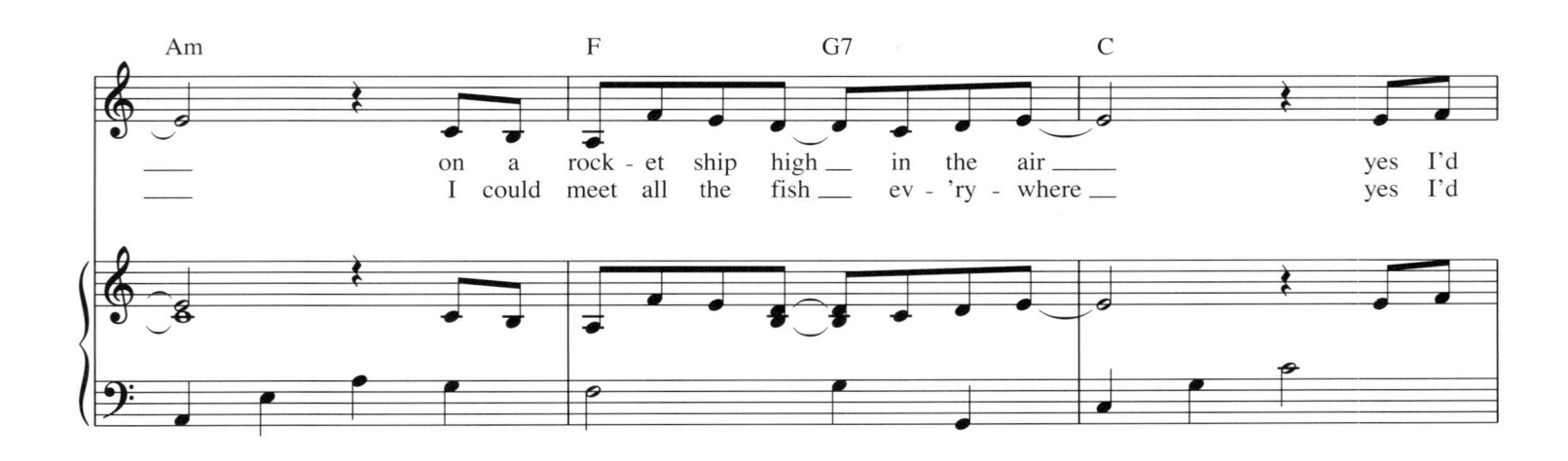

there. Though I'd like to look down at the earth from above soon I'd
there. I might stay for a day there if I had my wish. But there's

miss all the plac - es and peo - ple I love so al - though I might like it for
not much to do when your friends are all fish and an oy - ster and clam aren't

one af - ter - noon I don't want to live on the moon. I'd like to
real fam - i - ly so I don't want to live in the

sea. I'd like to vis - it the jun - gle hear the li - on roar go back in time __ and meet a di - no - saur. __ There's so man - y strange __ plac - es

I'd like to be ____ but none of them per - ma - nent - ly. So if

I should vis - it the moon __ well I'll dance on a moon - beam and then __

I will make a wish __ on a star ____ and I'll

wish I was home once a-gain. Though I'd like to look down at the earth from a-bove soon I'd miss all the plac-es and peo-ple I love so al-though I may go I'll be com-ing home soon 'cause I don't want to live on the moon. No I don't want to live on the moon.

I KNOW THINGS NOW
from *Into The Woods*

Words and Music by
Stephen Sondheim

Andante risoluto (♩ = 144)

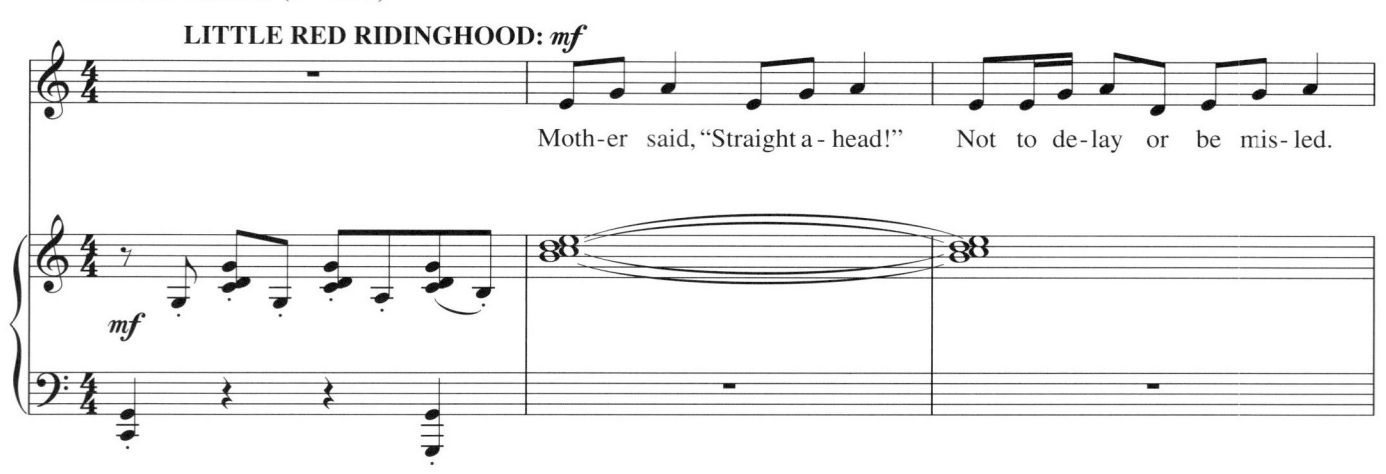

LITTLE RED RIDINGHOOD: *mf*

Moth-er said, "Straight a-head!" Not to de-lay or be mis-led.

I should have heed-ed her ad-vice... But he seemed so

nice. And he showed me things, man-y beau-ti-ful things, That I

© 1988 RILTING MUSIC, INC.
All Rights Administered by WB MUSIC CORP.
All Rights Reserved Used by Permission

had-n't thought to ex-plore. They were off my path, so I never had dared. I had been so care-ful I nev-er had cared. And he made me feel ex-cit-ed—well, ex-cit-ed and scared. When he said, "Come in!" with that sick-en-ing grin, How could I know what was in store?

Once his teeth were bared, though, I real-ly got scared— well, ex-cit-ed *and* scared— But he drew me close And he swal-lowed me down, Down a dark slim-y path where lie se-crets that I nev-er want to know. And when ev-'ry-thing fa-mil-iar seemed to dis-ap-pear for-ev-er, At the end of the path was

Gran-ny once a-gain! So we wait in the dark un-til some-one sets us free, And we're brought in-to the light, And we're back at the start. And I know things now, man-y val-ua-ble things, That I had-n't known be-fore: Do not put your faith in a cape and a hood, They will not pro-tect you the way that they should. And take ex-tra care with stran-gers, E-ven flow-ers have their dan-gers. And though scar-y is ex-cit-ing, Nice is dif-f'rent than good.

Now I know: don't be scared. Gran-ny is right, just be pre-pared. Is-n't it nice to know a lot!

And a lit-tle bit not...

I GOT THE SUN IN THE MORNING
from the Stage Production *Annie Get Your Gun*

Words and Music by
Irving Berlin

Light bounce

ANNIE:
Tak-ing stock of what I have and what I have-n't, what do I find? The things I've got will keep me sat-is-fied.

This song is performed by Annie, Ensemble and Dancers in the show, adapted here as a solo for Annie.

© Copyright 1946 by Irving Berlin
Copyright Renewed
International Copyright Secured   All Rights Reserved

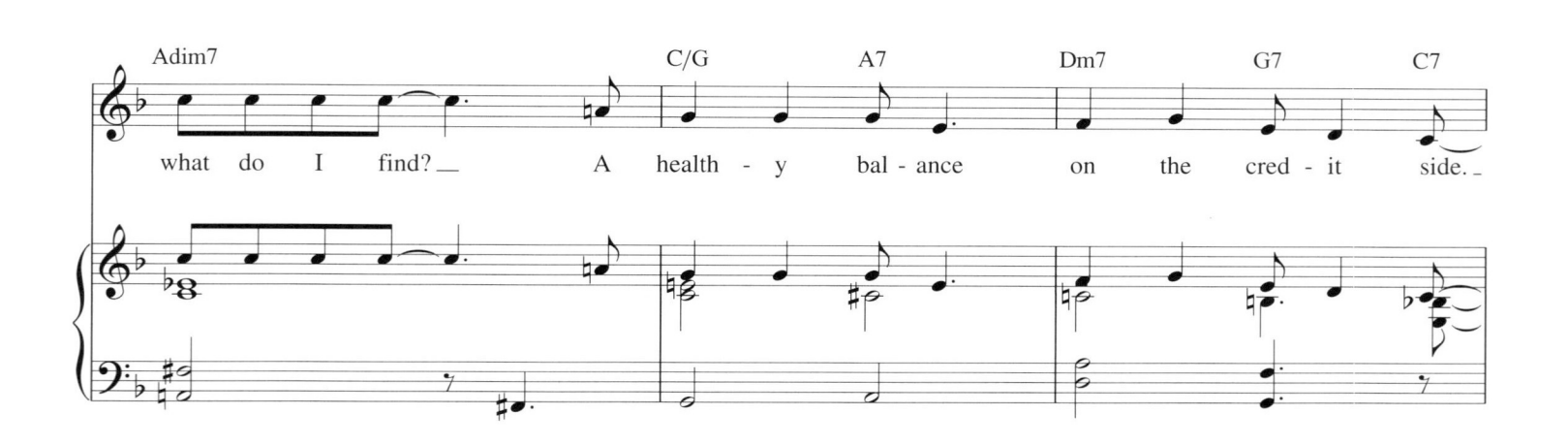

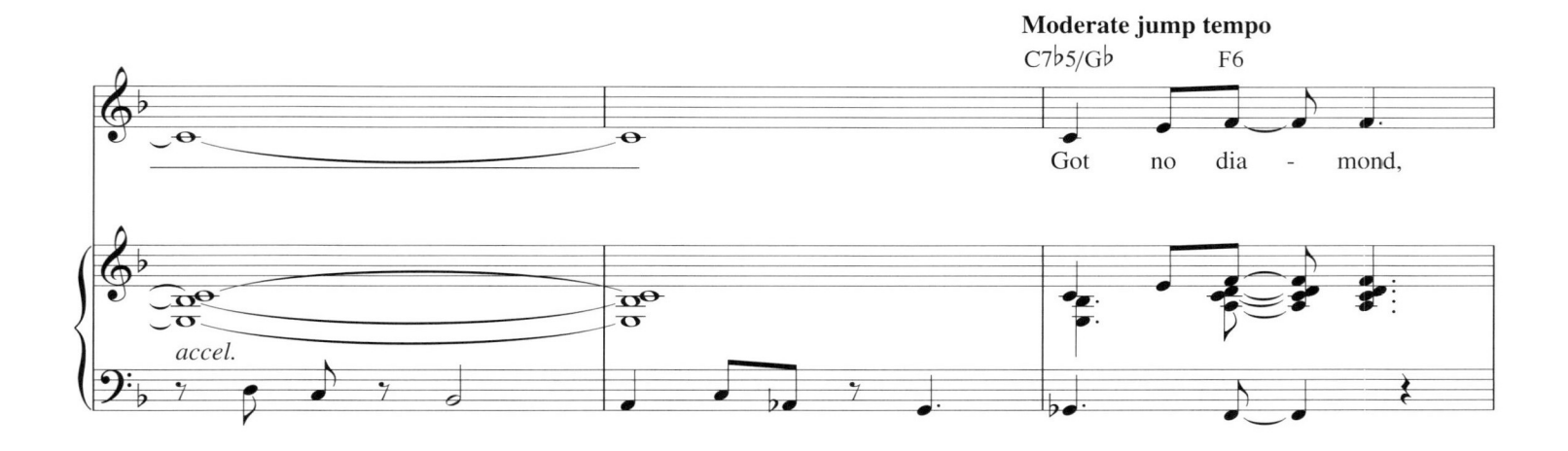

Checking up on what I have and what I haven't, what do I find? A healthy balance on the credit side.

Moderate jump tempo

Got no diamond, got no pearl, still I think I'm a lucky girl. I got the sun in the morn-ing and the moon at night.

Got no man-sion, got no yacht, still I'm hap-py with what I've got. I got the sun in the morn-ing and the moon at night.

Sun - shine _____ gives me a love - ly day. _____

Moon - light _____ gives me the Milk -

- y Way. _____ Got no check - books,

got no banks, _____ still I'd like _____ to ex -

Fmaj7 F7 B♭6/9 F/A
press my thanks. I got the sun in the morn - ing and the
Gm7 F6 B♭maj9 F(add9)/A
1
Gm7 F6
moon at night.
2
Gm7 F6 F7 B♭6/9 F/A
And with the sun in the morn - ing and the
A♭dim7 Gm7 C7♭9 F6 G♭7♯9 F6/9
moon in the eve - ning, I'm all right.

I WON'T GROW UP
from *Peter Pan*

Lyric by Carolyn Leigh
Music by Mark Charlap

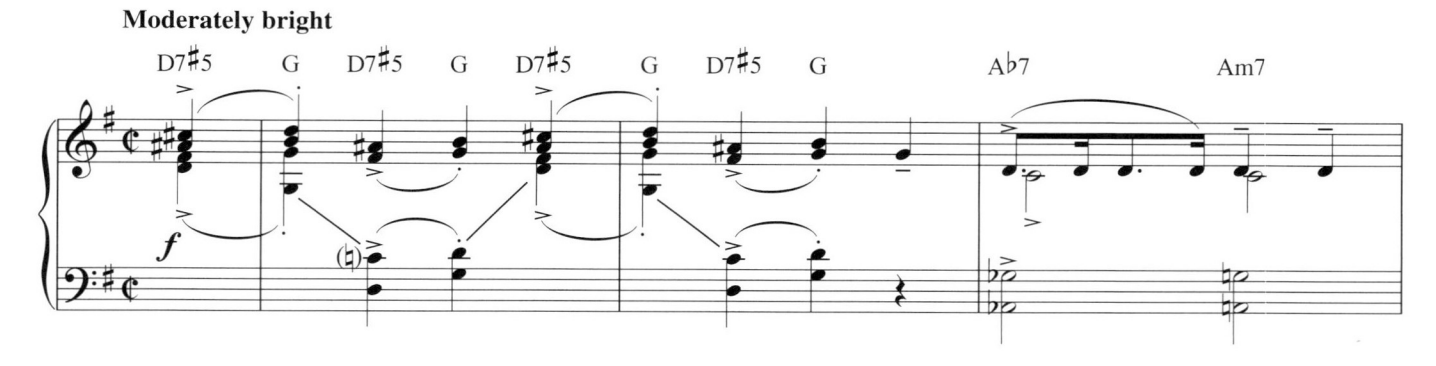

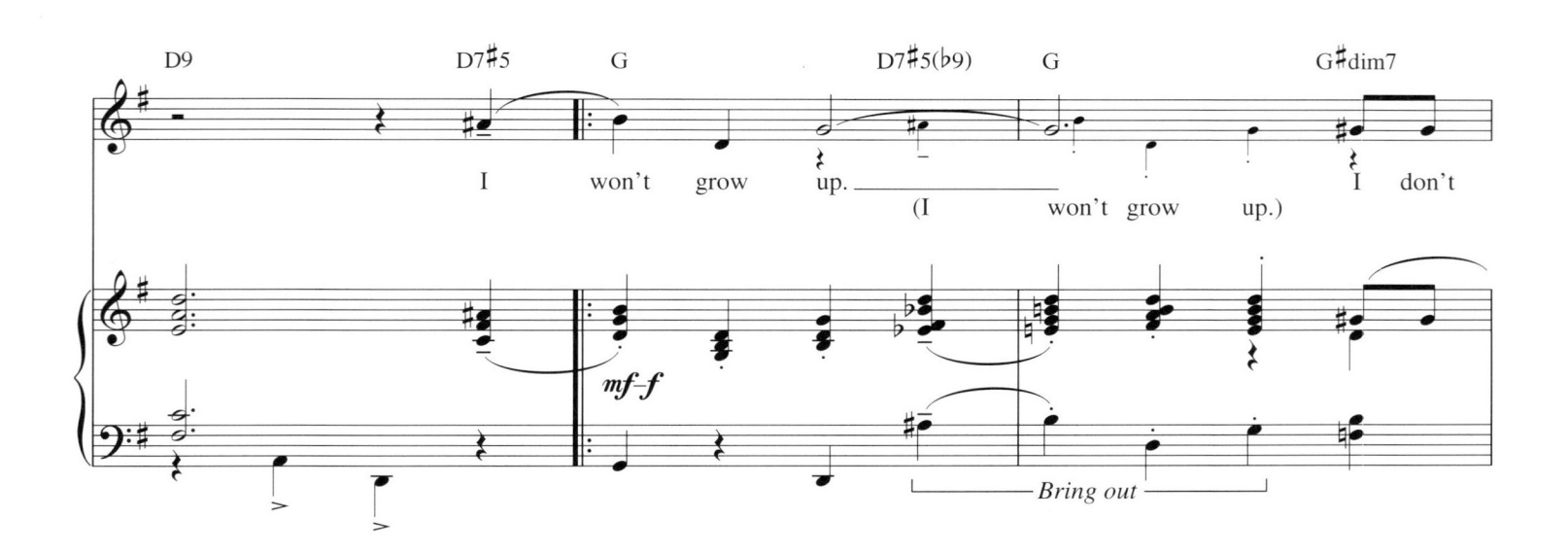

This song is performed by The Lost Boys in the show, adapted here as a solo.

© 1954 (Renewed 1982) CAROLYN LEIGH and MARK CHARLAP
All Rights Controlled by EDWIN H. MORRIS & COMPANY, A Division of MPL Music Publishing, Inc. and CARWIN MUSIC INC.
All Rights Reserved

Am7 D9 D7♯5 G D7♯5(♭9) G6 G7
and re - cite a sil - ly rule. If
learn to be a par - rot,) (and re - cite a sil - ly rule.)
Cmaj7 Cm6 Em7 B7♭9 E E7♭9
grow - ing up means it would be be - neath my dig - ni - ty to climb a tree, I'll
A9 Am7♭5 D7 D7♭9 G6 D7
nev - er grow up, nev - er grow up, nev - er grow up, not me! Not
G6 D7♭9 G6 D7 G6 D7♯5 G D7♯5(♭9)
I! Not me! Not me! I won't grow up. (I
8va
15ma
Bring

98

Am7♭5 D7 D7♭9 G6 D7 G6 D7♭9
grow up, nev - er grow up, so there! Not I! Not
8va
15ma
G6 D7 G6 G7 F♯dim7 G7 C
me! So there! Nev - er gon - na be a man,
(15ma)
D7 D7♯5(♭9) G C D7♯5(♭9) G
I won't! Like to see some-bod - y try and make me.
B7♭9 Em A7 D7sus
An - y - one who wants to try and make me turn in - to a man,

catch me if you can. I won't grow up. (I won't grow up.) Not a pen-ny will I pinch. (Not a pen-ny will I pinch.) I will nev-er grow a mus-tache (I will nev-er grow a mus-tache) or a frac-tion of an inch. (or a frac-tion of an inch.) 'Cause grow-ing up is aw-full-er than all the aw-ful things that ev - er were. I'll nev - er grow up, nev - er grow up, nev - er grow up, ___ no sir! Not I! Not me! No sir! I won't, no sir! I sir, not I, not me, I won't, no sir!

B♭(add9) B♭ B♭maj7 B♭6 B♭
fraid. While shiv - er - ing in my
B♭9 E♭ E♭maj7 E♭6
shoes I strike a care - less pose And
F7 F7♯5 B♭ N.C.
whis - tle a hap - py tune, And no one ev - er
F7 B♭6 B♭ Cm7/B♭ B♭/D
knows I'm a - fraid. The re -
mp

sult of this de-cep-tion is ver-y strange to tell For when I fool the peo-ple I fear, I fool my-self as well! I whis-tle a hap-py tune And ev-'ry sin-gle time The hap - pi - ness in the tune con - vinc - es me that

I'm not a - fraid.

Coda

Make be - lieve you're brave And the trick will take you far.

You may be as brave as you make be - lieve you

are. Whistle _____

You may be as brave as you make believe you

are.

I'D DO ANYTHING
from the Broadway Musical *Oliver!*

Words and Music by
Lionel Bart

I'd do anything for you, dear, anything, for you mean ev'rything to me. I know that I'd go

This song is performed by The Artful Dodger, Nancy, Oliver Twist, Bet and Fagin in the show, adapted here as a solo.

© Copyright 1960 (Renewed) Lakeview Music Co., Ltd., London, England
TRO - Hollis Music, Inc., New York, controls all publication rights for the U.S.A. and Canada
International Copyright Secured
All Rights Reserved Including Public Performance For Profit
Used by Permission

108

anywhere for your smile, anywhere, for your smile ev-'ry-where I'd see.

Would you lace my shoe? An-y-thing! Paint your face bright blue? An-y-thing! Catch a kan-ga-roo?
Would you rob a shop? An-y-thing! Would you risk "the drop"? An-y-thing! Tho' your eyes go "pop"?

*When singing this song as a solo, this phrase in parentheses should probably be omitted.

I'M LATE
from Walt Disney's *Alice in Wonderland*

Words by Bob Hilliard
Music by Sammy Fain

Brightly

THE WHITE RABBIT:

I'm late, I'm late for a ver-y im-por-tant date. No time to say hel-lo, good-bye, I'm late, I'm late, I'm late, I'm late, and when I wave, I lose the time I save. My fuzz-y ears and

© 1949 Walt Disney Music Company
Copyright Renewed
All Rights Reserved   Used by Permission

whis-kers took me too much time to shave. I run and then I hop, hop, hop; I wish that I could fly. There's dan-ger if I dare to stop and here's the rea-son why (you see) I'm o-ver-due; I'm in a rab-bit stew. Can't e-ven say good-bye, hel-lo, I'm late, I'm late, I'm late.

I'VE GOT NO STRINGS

from Walt Disney's *Pinocchio*

Words by Ned Washington
Music by Leigh Harline

Copyright © 1940 by Bourne Co. (ASCAP)
Copyright Renewed
International Copyright Secured All Rights Reserved

C7 C C7(♯5) F6 C7
me, not me; you see, I've got no strings so I have fun, I'm
mf
F6 C7 Gm7sus4 B♭/C A7/C♯
not tied up to an - y one! How I love my li - ber - ty, there are no strings on
Dm Csus4(9) C7 D♭7
me! There are no strings! I said no strings! I've
f
subito p
f
subito p
Gm7sus4 C F
got no strings on me!
cresc.
sfz

IN MY OWN LITTLE CORNER

from *Cinderella*

Lyrics by Oscar Hammerstein II
Music by Richard Rodgers

corner, in my own little chair, I can be what-
ever I want to be. On the wing of my
fancy I can fly anywhere And the world will
open its arms to me. I'm a young Norwegian

princess or a milkmaid, ____ I'm the greatest prima donna in Milan. ____ I'm an heiress who has always had her silk made ____ By her own flock of silkworms in Japan. ____ I'm a girl men go mad for, love's a game I can play with a cool and con-fi-dent kind of air, _____ Just as long as I stay in my own lit-tle cor - ner, _____ All a-lone in my own lit-tle chair. In my chair. _____

IT'S THE HARD-KNOCK LIFE

from the Musical Production *Annie*

Lyric by Martin Charnin
Music by Charles Strouse

Moderately with a tough edge

ANNIE:

It's the hard-knock life for us! It's the hard-knock life for us!

'Stead-a treated ___ we get tricked, 'Stead-a kisses ___ we get kicked,

It's the hard-knock ___ life! Got no folks to speak of, so, ___

This song is performed by Annie and The Orphans in the show, adapted here as a solo for Annie.

© 1977 (Renewed) EDWIN H. MORRIS & COMPANY, A Division of MPL Music Publishing, Inc. and CHARLES STROUSE
All Rights on behalf of CHARLES STROUSE owned by CHARLES STROUSE PUBLISHING (Administered by WILLIAMSON MUSIC)
All Rights Reserved   Used by Permission
www.CharlesStrouse.com

it's the hard-knock row we hoe. Cot-ton blan-kets 'stead-a wool,
emp-ty bel-lies 'stead-a full, it's the hard-knock life.
Don't it feel like the wind is al-ways howl-in'? Don't it
seem like there's nev-er an-y light? Once a day don't you want to throw the

towel in? It's eas-i-er than put-tin' up a fight. No one's there when your dreams at night get creep-y, No one cares if you grow, or if you shrink, no one dries when your eyes get wet and weep-y. From the cry-in' you would think this place would sink. Oh!

Santa Claus we nev-er see, Santa Claus, what's that? Who's he?

No one cares for you a smidge when you're in an or-phan-idge,

It's the hard-knock life (Yes it is) It's the hard-knock

life. (Yes it is) It's the hard-knock life.

JOIN THE CIRCUS
from *Barnum*

Music by Cy Coleman
Lyrics by Michael Stewart
Arranged by Michael Dansicker

Steady "2" ♩ = 138

When the pill the doctor gave you turns your cold to the grippe, When a stitch to save nine others comes a-part with a rip, When the rats in-vade your at-tic, and start leav-ing your ship,

This song is an ensemble number in the show, adapted here as a solo.

Copyright © 1980 Notable Music Company, Inc.
All Rights Administered by Chrysalis Music
All Rights Reserved Used by Permission

B♭7
B♭7 A♭/C B♭7/D
E♭7(add6)
E♭7
Fol - low my tip, Come a - way on a trip! Just
mf
Circus Feel
A♭ A♭maj7 A♭6 A♭ B♭9
join the cir - cus like you want - ed to When you
B♭9(add6) B♭ E♭7 B♭7/D
were a kid. Climb a - board be -
E♭7 E♭7/D♭ E♭7/C E♭7/B♭ A♭/C E 7/B E♭7/B♭ B♭7 E♭7
fore it moves on and you'll Thank your luck - y stars you did.

Go to bed in Minneapolis, Wake up in P. A. Pack your roll, your brush and your comb again, Ready to roam again, Ready to stray. Bless your soul, you'll never go home

— a-gain, When the cir - cus comes your way.

Run a - way!

LES POISSONS
from Walt Disney's *The Little Mermaid*

Music by Alan Menken
Lyrics by Howard Ashman

Bright Waltz

CHEF LOUIS:
Les Pois-sons, les pois-sons, how I love les pois-sons, love to chop and to serve lit-tle fish. First I cut off their heads, then I

© 1988 Wonderland Music Company, Inc. and Walt Disney Music Company
All Rights Reserved   Used by Permission

pull out their bones. Ah mais oui, ca c'est tou-jours de-lish.

Les pois-sons, les pois-sons, hee hee hee, hah hah hah.

With the cleav-er I hack them in two. I pull

out what's in-side and I serve it up fried. Oh, I

love lit-tle fish-es, don't you? Here's some-thing for tempt-ing the pal-ate, Pre-pared in the clas-sic tech-nique. First you pound the fish flat with a mal-let. Then you slash through the skin, give the bel-ly a

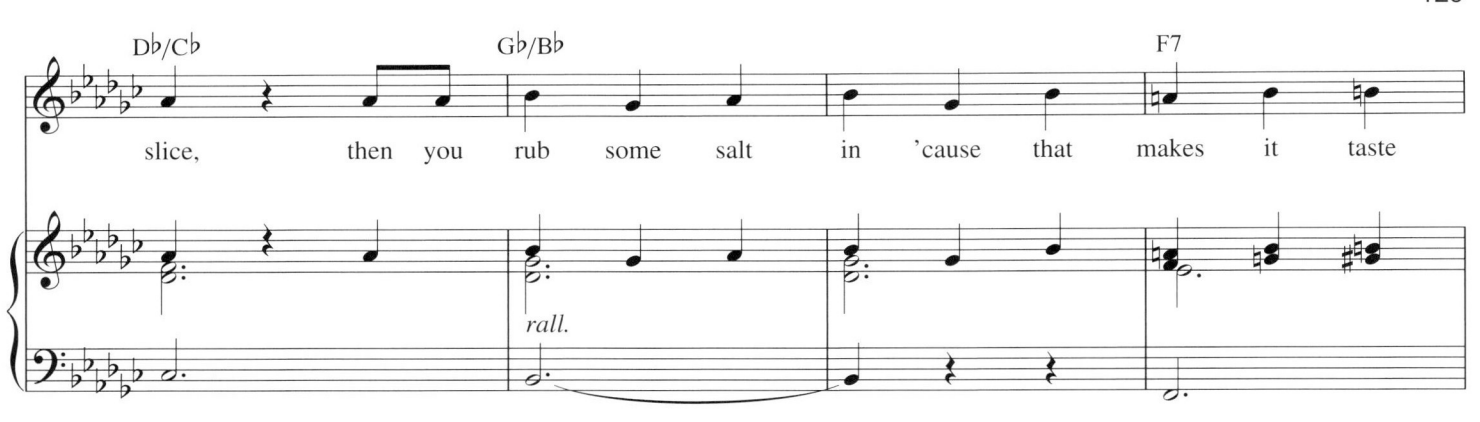

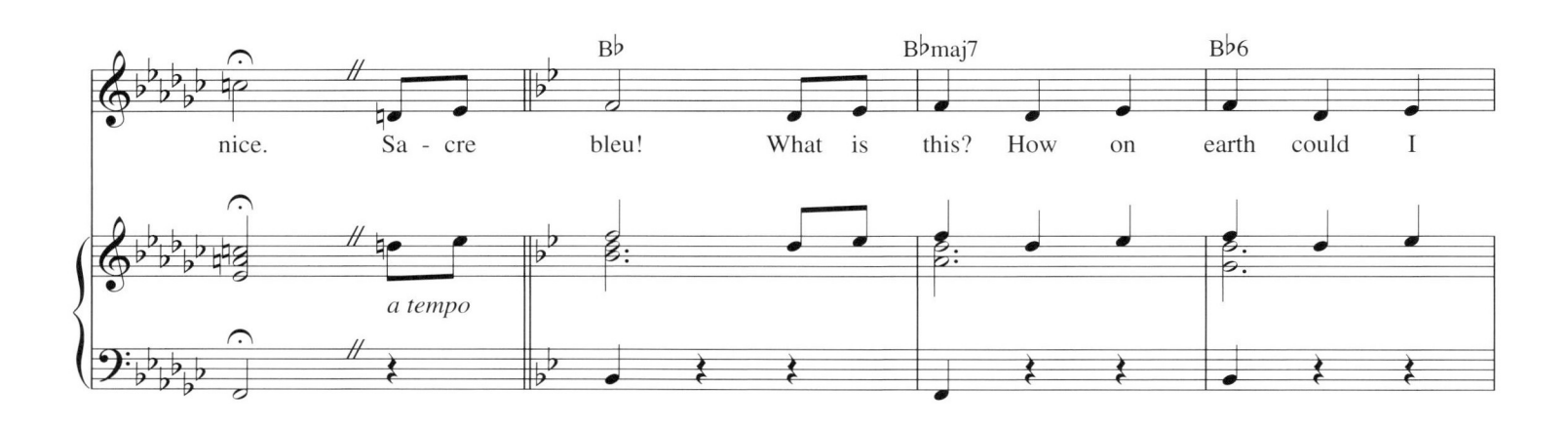

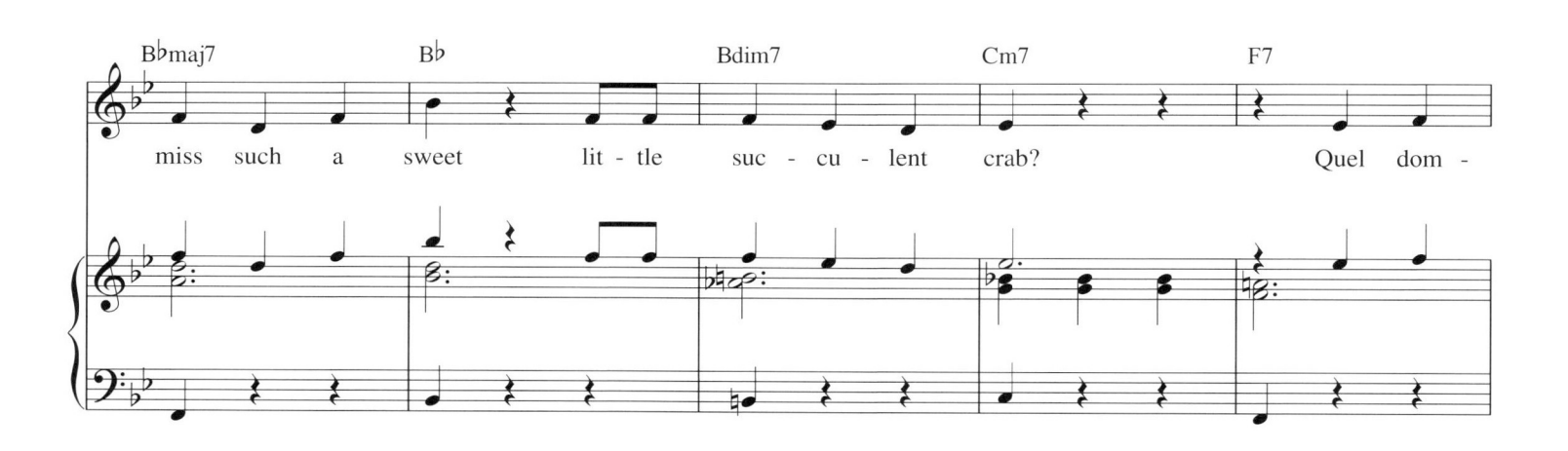

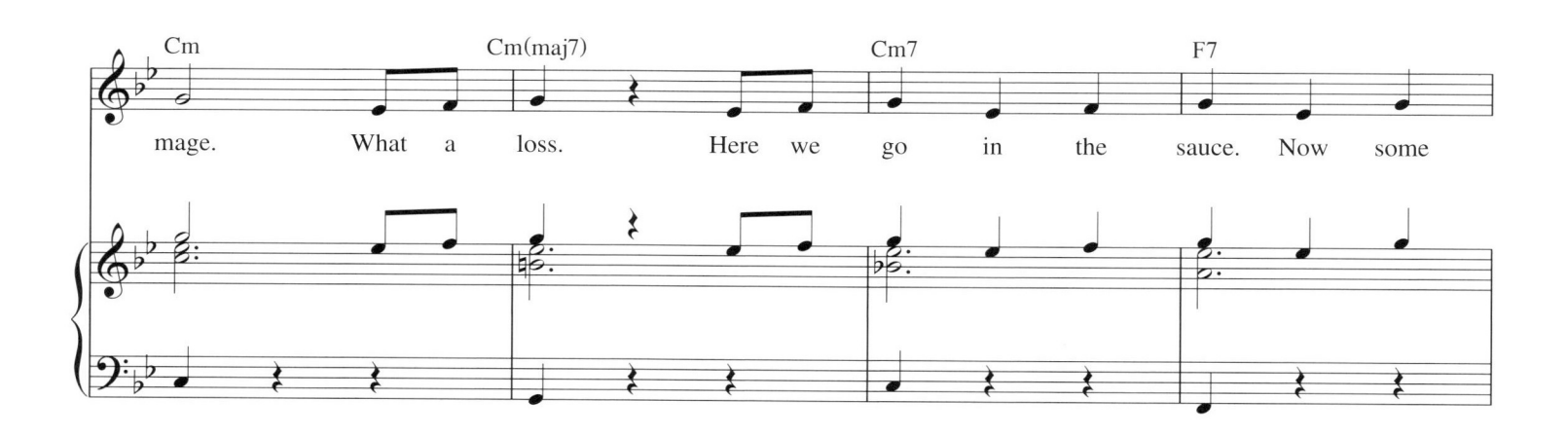

slice, then you rub some salt in 'cause that makes it taste nice. Sacre bleu! What is this? How on earth could I miss such a sweet little succulent crab? Quel dommage. What a loss. Here we go in the sauce. Now some flour__ I think, just a dab. Now I stuff you with bread. It don't hurt 'cause you're dead. And you're cer-tain-ly luck-y you are. 'Cause it's gon-na be hot in my big sil-ver pot. Too-dle loo, mon pois-son, au re-voir!

LET ME ENTERTAIN YOU
from *Gypsy*

Words by Stephen Sondheim
Music by Jule Styne

Moderate Waltz

JUNE:
Let me en-ter-tain you. Let me make you smile. I will do some kicks. I will do some tricks.

This song is performed by June and Louise in the show, adapted here as a solo for June.

© 1959 (Renewed) STRATFORD MUSIC CORPORATION and WILLIAMSON MUSIC CO.
All Rights Administered by CHAPPELL & CO., INC.
All Rights Reserved   Used by Permission

I'll tell you a sto-ry. I'll dance when I'm done. By the time I'm through en-ter-tain-ing you, You'll have a bar-rel of fun.

Moderately (with a lilt and not fast)

Let me en-ter-tain you, let me make you smile. Let me do a few tricks, some old and then some new tricks; I'm ver - y ver - sa - tile.

And if you're real good, I'll make you feel good, I want your spir - its to climb. Just let me en - ter - tain you, and we'll have a real good time, yes sir, we'll have a real good time.

LET'S GO FLY A KITE
from Walt Disney's *Mary Poppins*

Words and Music by Richard M. Sherman and Robert B. Sherman

With tuppence for paper and strings, You can have your own set of wings;
With your feet on the ground, you're a bird in flight
With your fist holding tight to the string of your

Send it flying up there, All at once you're lighter than air;
You can dance on the breeze over houses and trees
With your fist holding tight to the string of your

This song is performed as an ensemble in the film, adapted here as a solo.

© 1963 Wonderland Music Company, Inc.
Copyright Renewed
All Rights Reserved   Used by Permission

B♭
cresc.
B♭7
E♭
f
kite.
kite.
Oh!
Let's
cresc.
f
B♭
go fly a kite Up to the
D♭dim
F7
Cm7
high - est height! Let's go fly a
F7
B♭
Cm7
C♯dim
B♭
kite And send it soar - ing

Up through the at-mos-phere, Up where the air is clear. Oh, let's go fly a kite! When you kite!

LITTLE LAMB
from *Gypsy*

Words by Stephen Sondheim
Music by Jule Styne

Gently

LOUISE: Little lamb, little lamb, My birthday is here at last. Little lamb, little lamb, A birthday goes by so fast. Little bear, little bear, You

sit on my right, right there. Little hen, little hen, What game should we play, and when? Little cat, little cat, Ah, why do you look so blue? Did somebody paint you like that, Or is it your birthday too? Little fish, little fish, Do you think I'll get my wish? Little lamb, little lamb, I wonder how old I am. I wonder how old I am. Little am. am.

LITTLE PEOPLE
from *Les Misérables*

Music by Claude-Michel Schönberg
Lyrics by Alain Boublil, Jean-Marc Natel
and Herbert Kretzmer

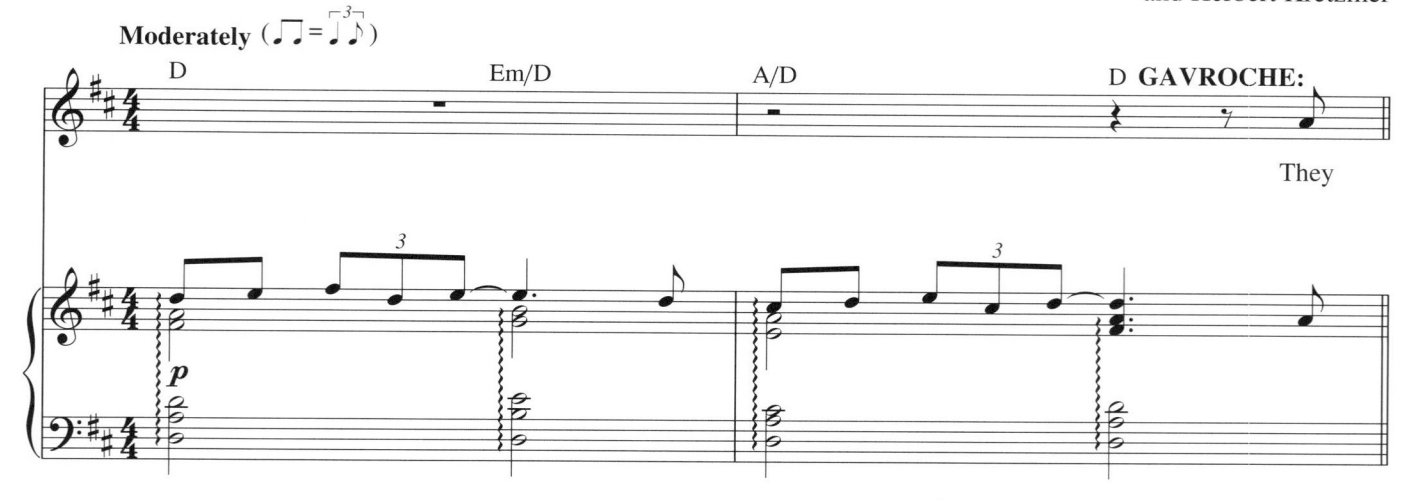

GAVROCHE:
They laugh at me, these fellows, just because I am small. They
Goliath was a bruiser who was tall as the sky. But

laugh at me because I'm not a hundred feet tall! I
David threw a right and gave him one in the eye. I

Music and Lyrics Copyright © 1980 by Editions Musicales Alain Boublil
English Lyrics Copyright © 1986 by Alain Boublil Music Ltd. (ASCAP)
Mechanical and Publication Rights for the U.S.A. Administered by Alain Boublil Music Ltd. (ASCAP)
c/o Joel Faden & Co., Inc., MLM 250 West 57th Street, 26th Floor, New York, NY 10107, Tel. (212) 246-7203, Fax (212) 246-7217, Email mwlock@joelfaden.com
International Copyright Secured. All Rights Reserved. This music is copyright. Photocopying is illegal.
All Performance Rights Restricted.

tell 'em there's a lot to learn down here on the ground. The
nev-er read the Bi-ble but I know that it's true. It

world is big but lit-tle peo-ple turn it a-round.
on-ly goes to show what lit-tle peo-ple can do!

worm can roll a stone, a bee can sting a bear, a

fly can fly a-round Ver-sailles 'cos flies don't care!

sparrow in a hat can make a happy home, a flea can bite the bottom of the Pope in Rome! Go - Pope in Rome!

So listen here, Professor, with your head in the cloud, it's often kind of useful to get lost in a crowd.

So keep your u-ni-ver-si-ties, I don't give a damn; for better or for worse it is the way that I am! Be careful as you go 'cos little people grow... And little people know when little people fight we may look eas-y pick-ings but we got some bite! So nev-er kick a dog be-cause it's just a pup. You bet-ter run for cov-er when the pup grows up! And we'll fight like twen-ty ar-mies and we won't give up! A

CODA

flea can bite the bot-tom of the Pope in Rome!

MAYBE
from the Musical Production *Annie*

Lyric by Martin Charnin
Music by Charles Strouse

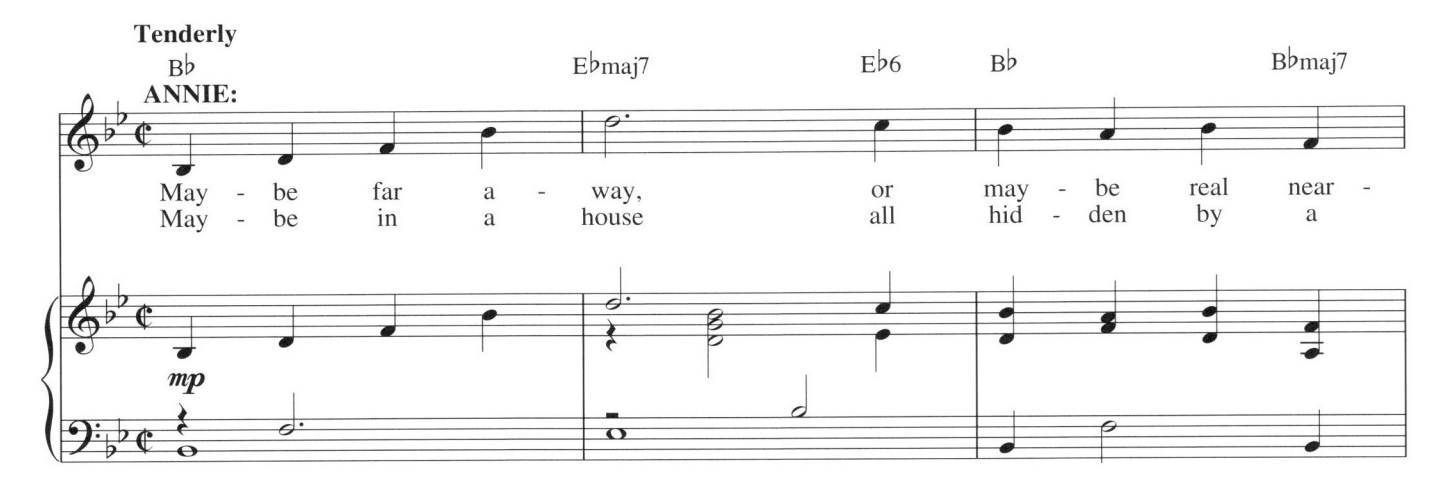

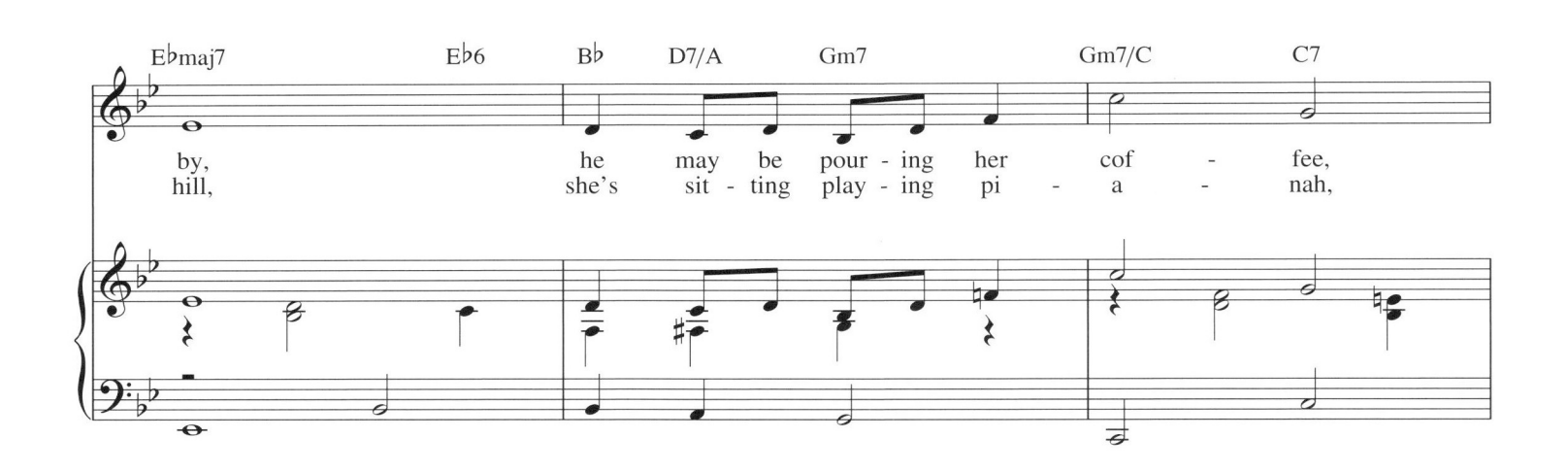

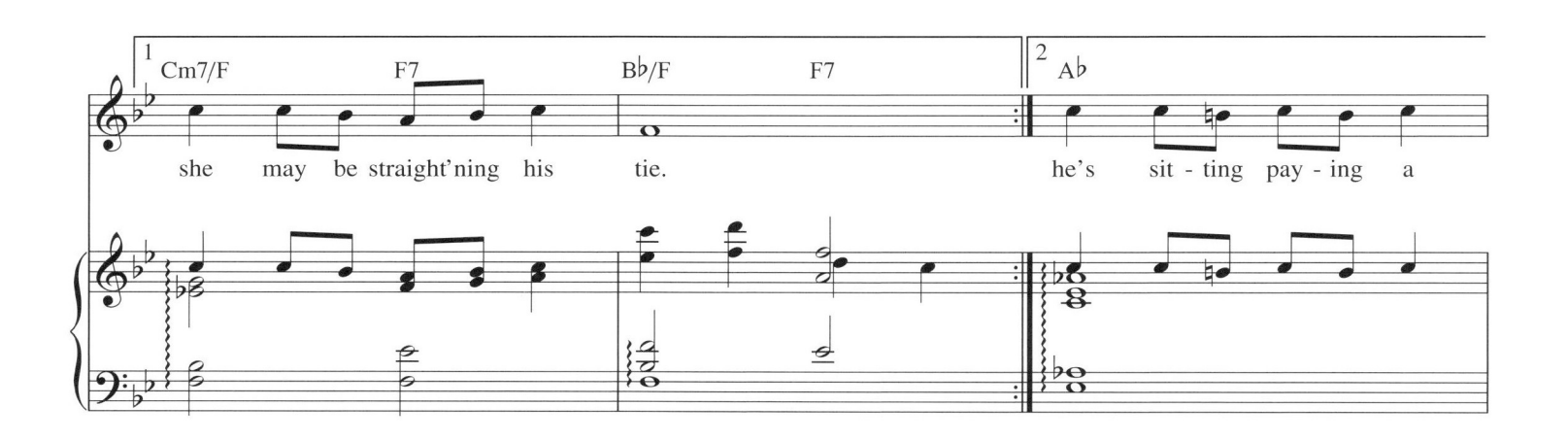

Tenderly

ANNIE:
May - be far a - way, or may - be real near - by,
May - be in a house all hid - den by a hill,

he may be pour - ing her cof - fee,
she's sit - ting play - ing pi - a - nah,

1. she may be straight'ning his tie.
2. he's sit - ting pay - ing a

© 1977 (Renewed) EDWIN H. MORRIS & COMPANY, A Division of MPL Music Publishing, Inc. and CHARLES STROUSE
All rights on behalf of CHARLES STROUSE owned by CHARLES STROUSE PUBLISHING (Administered by WILLIAMSON MUSIC,
a Division of Rodgers & Hammerstein: an Imagem Company)
All Rights Reserved   Used by Permission
www.CharlesStrouse.com

bill. Bet - cha they're young, _ bet - cha they're smart, _
Bet - cha he reads, _ bet - cha she sews, _

bet they col - lect _ things like ash - trays and art. _
may - be she's made _ me a clos - et of clothes. _

Bet - cha they're good, _ why should - n't they be,
May - be they're strict, _ as straight as a line. _

their one mis - take was giv - ing up me. _
Don't real - ly care as long as they're mine. _

B♭
E♭maj7
E♭6
So, may - be now it's time, and
So, may - be now this prayer's the
B♭
B♭maj7
E♭maj7
E♭6
B♭
D7/A
Gm7
may - be when I wake they'll be there call - ing me
last one of its kind: Won't you please come get your
Gm7/C
C7
1
Cm7
F7
B♭/F
E7
"Ba - by," may - be.
ba - by,
2
Cm7
F7
B♭
E♭maj7
B♭
may - be.

MY BEST GIRL (MY BEST BEAU)
from *Mame*

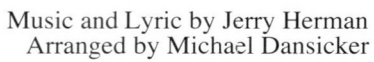

Music and Lyric by Jerry Herman
Arranged by Michael Dansicker

Moderate Waltz

You're my best girl and noth-ing you do is wrong, I'm proud you be-long to me; And if a day is rough for me, Hav-ing you there's e-nough for me. And if some-day an-

(beau)*

---

* This may be used as a substitute throughout.
This song is performed by Patrick and Mame Dennis in the show, adapted here as a solo.

© 1966 (Renewed) JERRY HERMAN
All Rights Controlled by Jerryco Music Co.
Exclusive Agent: EDWIN H. MORRIS & COMPANY, A Division of MPL Music Publishing, Inc.
All Rights Reserved

oth-er girl comes a-long, It won't take her long to see, That I'll still be found just hangin' a-round My best girl. And if some-day an-oth-er girl comes a-long, It won't take her long to see, _____ That I'll still be found _____ just hang-in' a-round _____ MY BEST GIRL! _____ MY BEST GIRL. _____

ON THE GOOD SHIP LOLLIPOP
from *Bright Eyes*

Words and Music by Sidney Clare
and Richard A. Whiting

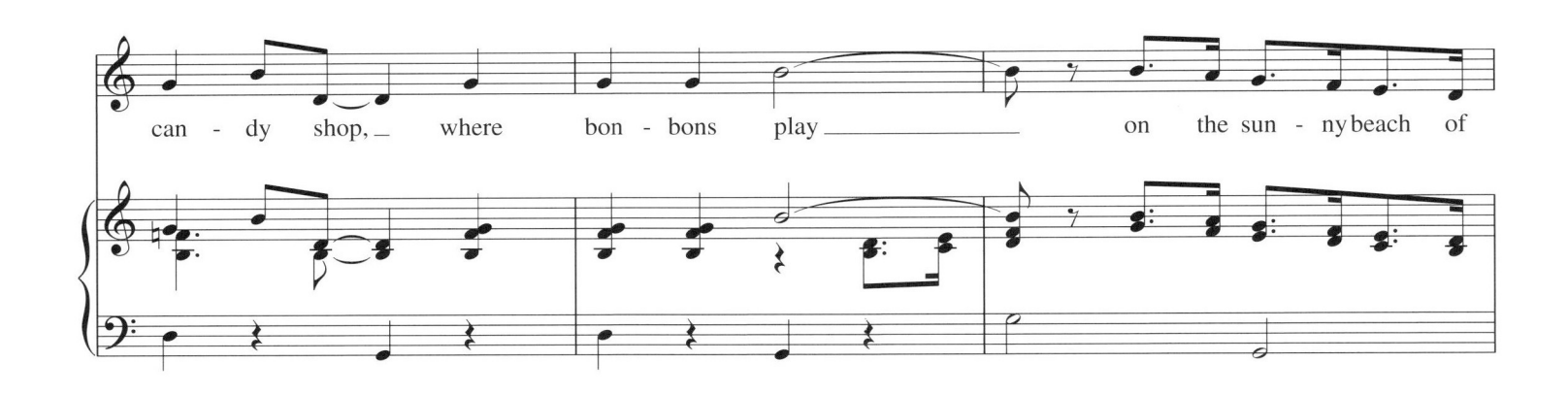

Lightly

SHIRLEY:
On the good ship, Lol-li-pop, it's a sweet trip to a can-dy shop, where bon-bons play on the sun-ny beach of pep-per-mint bay. Lem-on-ade stands

© 1934 (Renewed 1962) EMI APRIL MUSIC INC. and BOURNE CO. (ASCAP)
All Rights Reserved   International Copyright Secured   Used by Permission

ev - 'ry - where, crack - er - jack bands fill the air, and there you are happy land - ing on a choc - o - late bar. See the sug - ar bowl do a toot - sie roll with the big bad dev - il's food cake. If you eat too much, ooh! ooh! you'll a-wake with a tum-my ache. On the good ship, Lol-li-pop, it's a night trip into bed you hop with this com-mand: "All a-board for and dream a-way on the good ship, Can-dy Land." On the Lol-li-pop!

MY FAVORITE THINGS
from *The Sound of Music*

Lyrics by Oscar Hammerstein II
Music by Richard Rodgers

Allegro animato

MARIA:
Rain-drops on ros-es and whis-kers on kit-tens, Bright cop-per ket-tles and warm wool-en mit-tens, Brown pa-per pack-ages tied up with strings, These are a few of my fa-vor-ite things.

Copyright © 1959 by Richard Rodgers and Oscar Hammerstein II
Copyright Renewed
Williamson Music, a Division of Rodgers & Hammerstein: an Imagem Company, owner of publication and allied rights throughout the world
International Copyright Secured   All Rights Reserved

Cream-colored ponies and crisp apple strudels, Doorbells and sleighbells and schnitzel with noodles, Wild geese that fly with the moon on their wings, These are a few of my favorite things.

Girls in white dress-es with blue sat-in sash-es, Snow-flakes that stay on my nose and eye-lash-es, Sil-ver white win-ters that melt in-to springs, These are a few of my fa-vor-ite things.

When the dog bites, When the bee stings, When I'm

feel-ing sad, _____ I sim-ply re-mem-ber my fa-vor-ite things and then I don't feel so bad. bad. _____

PART OF YOUR WORLD
from Walt Disney's *The Little Mermaid*

Music by Alan Menken
Lyrics by Howard Ashman

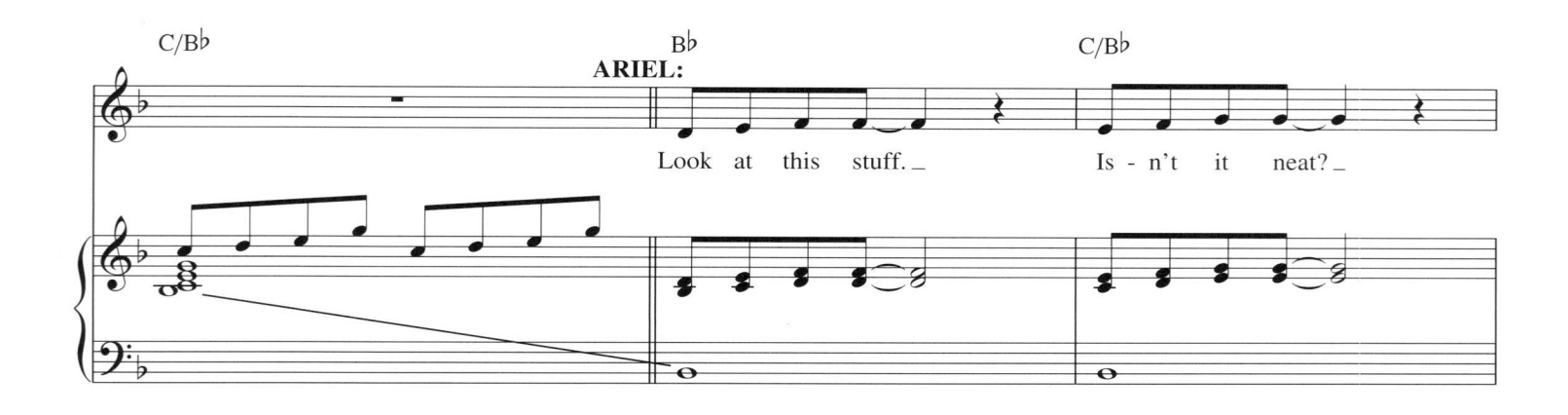

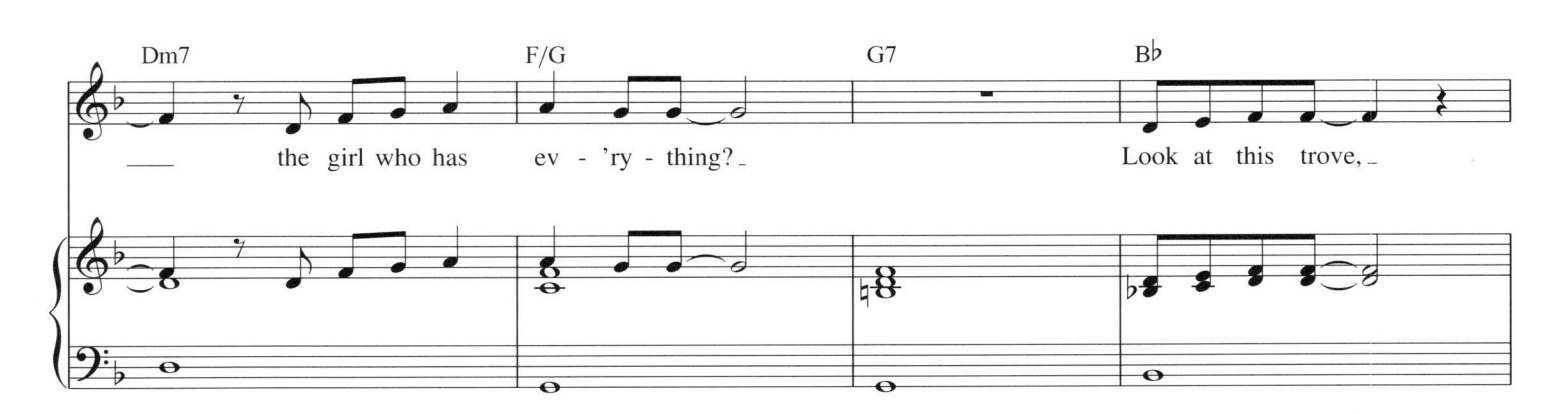

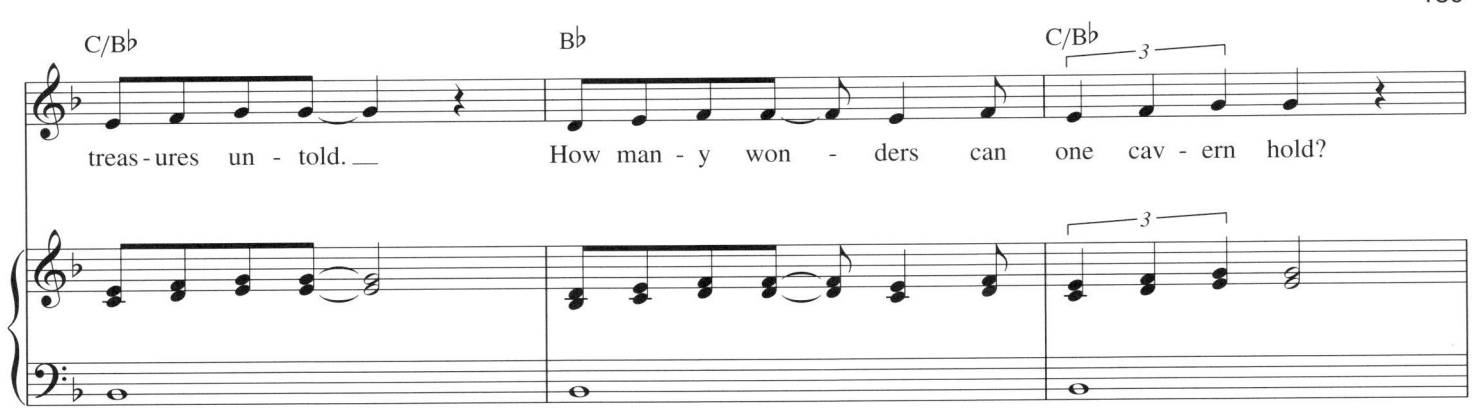

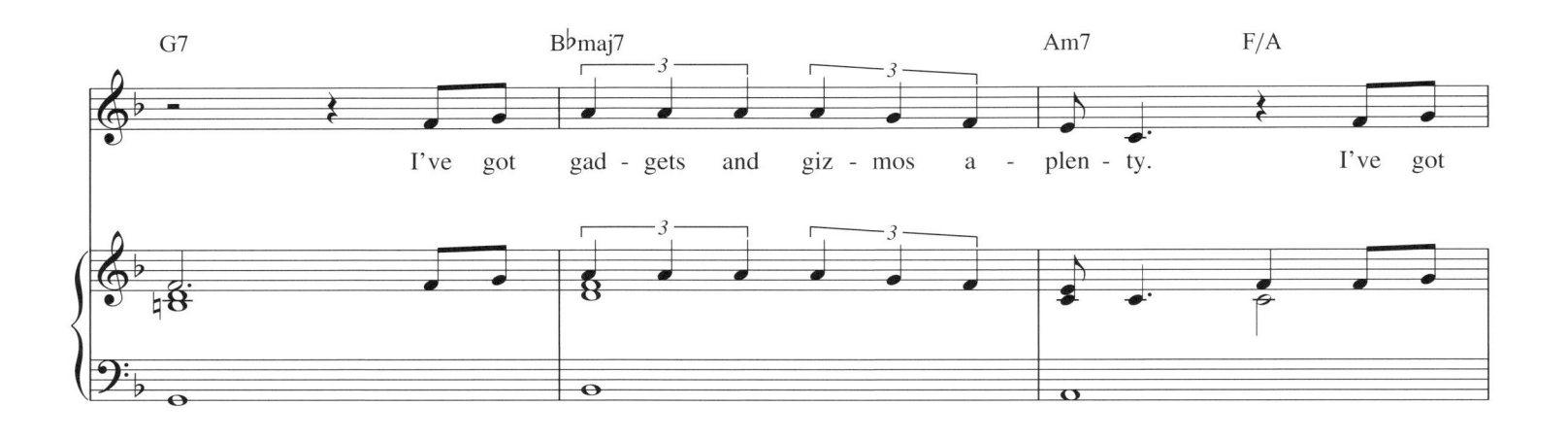

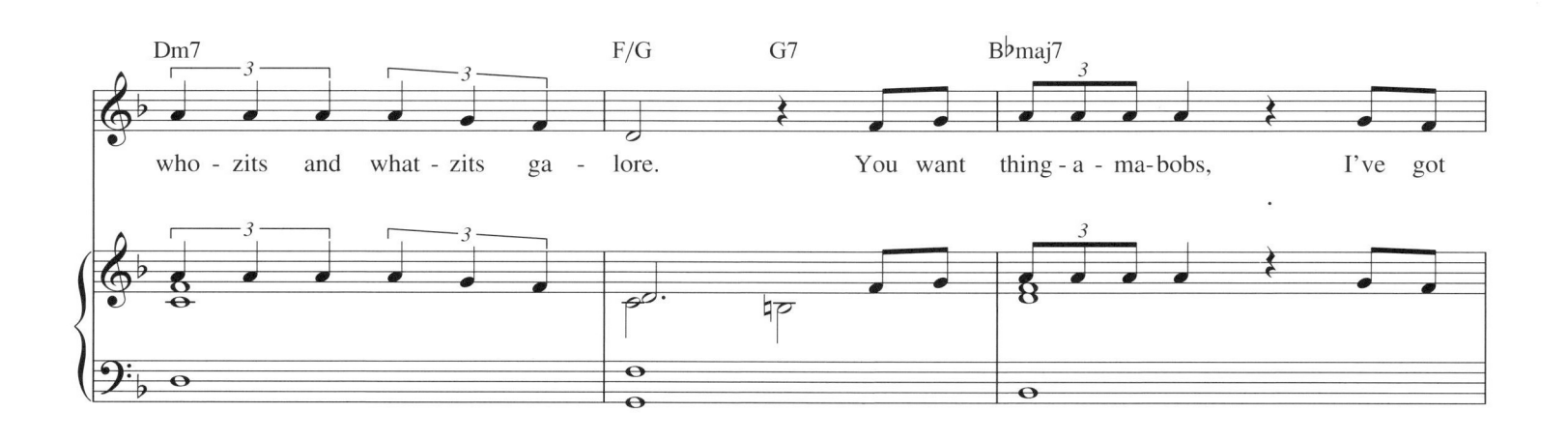

treas-ures un-told. How man-y won-ders can one cav-ern hold?

Look-ing a-round here you'd think, sure, she's got ev-'ry-thing.

I've got gad-gets and giz-mos a-plen-ty. I've got

who-zits and what-zits ga-lore. You want thing-a-ma-bobs, I've got twen-ty. But who cares? No big deal. I want more.

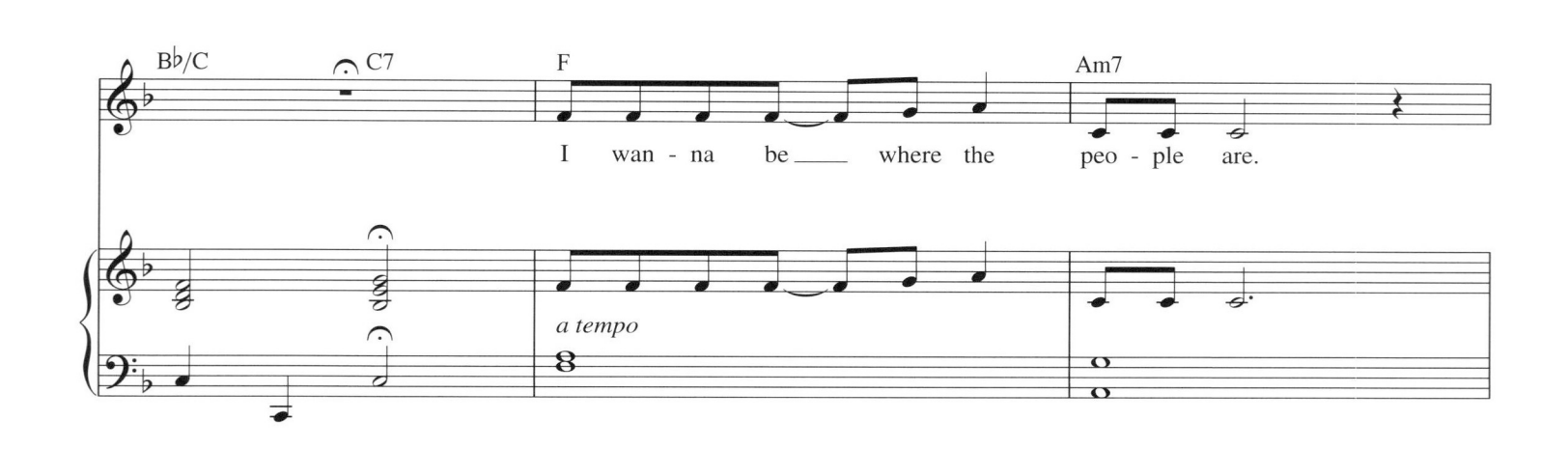

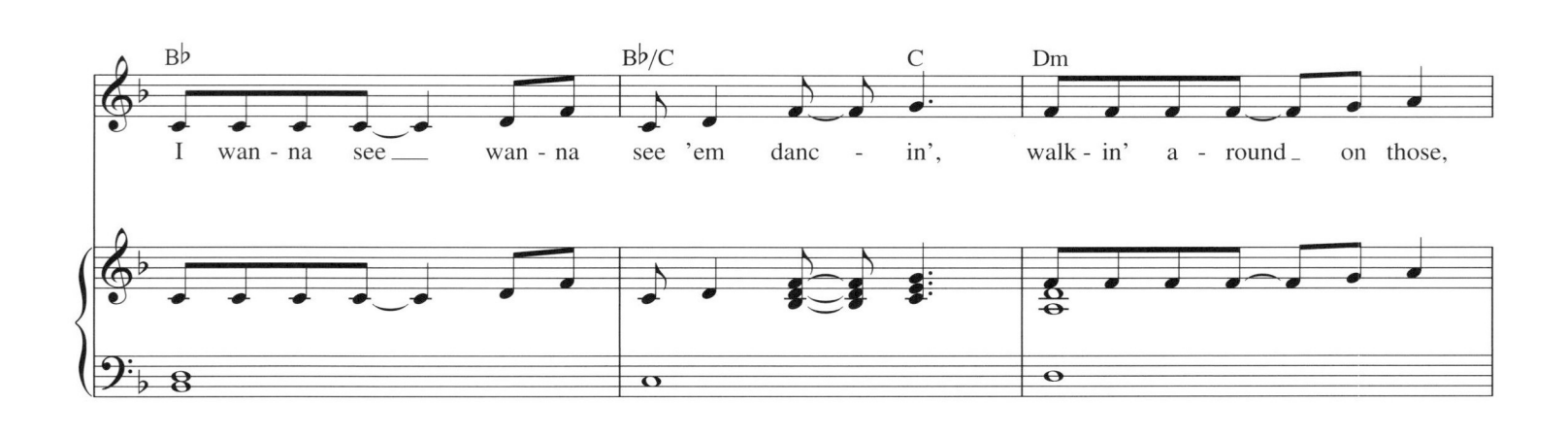

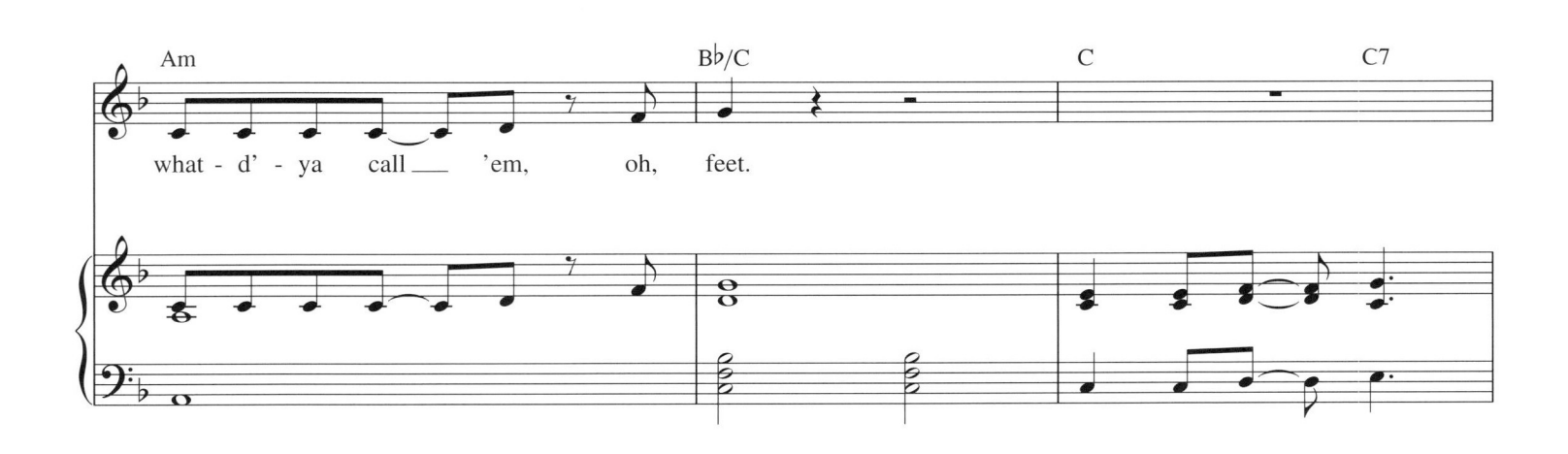

I wan-na be where the peo-ple are.

I wan-na see, wan-na see 'em danc-in', walk-in' a-round on those,

what-d'-ya call 'em, oh, feet.

Flip-pin' your fins you don't get too far. Legs are re-quired for jump-in', danc-in'. Stroll-in' a-long down the, what's that word a-gain, street. Up where they walk, up where they run, up where they stay all day in the sun. Wan-der-in' free, wish I could

be part of that world. What would I give if I could live outta these waters. What would I pay to spend a day warm on the sand. Betcha on land they understand. Bet they don't reprimand their daughters. Bright young

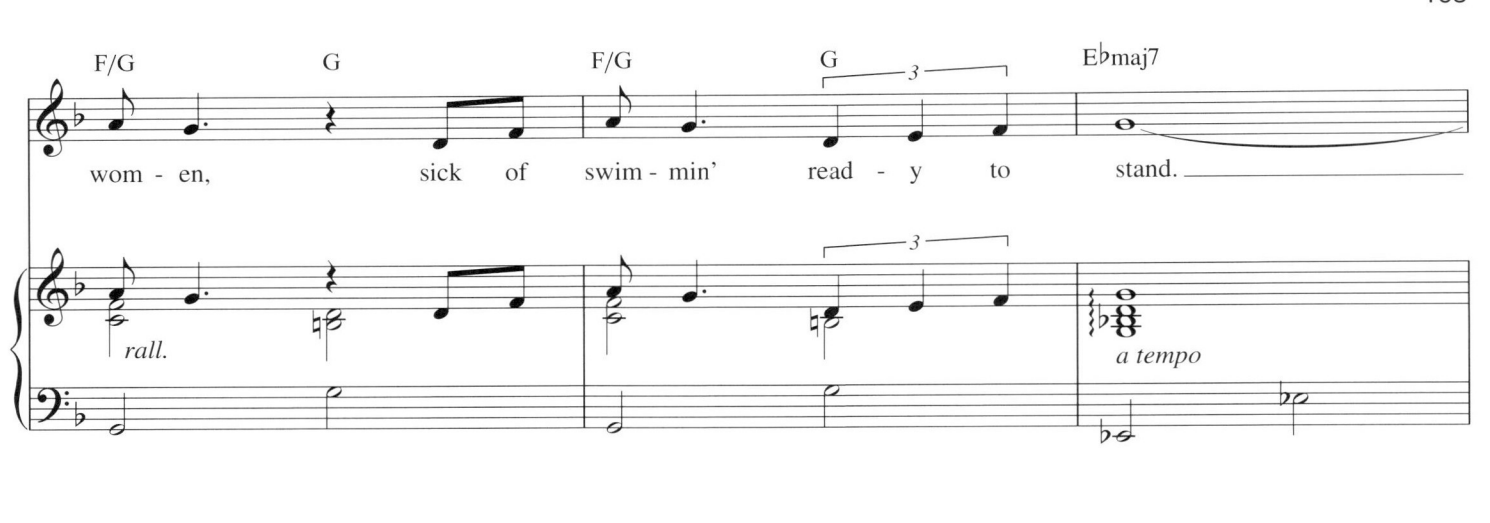

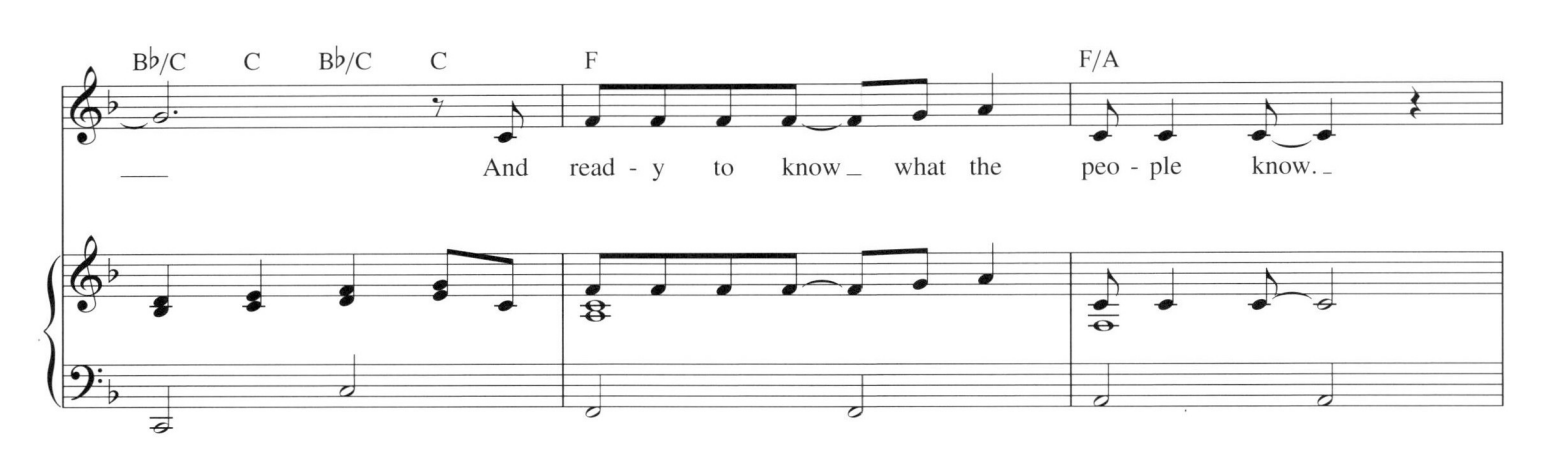

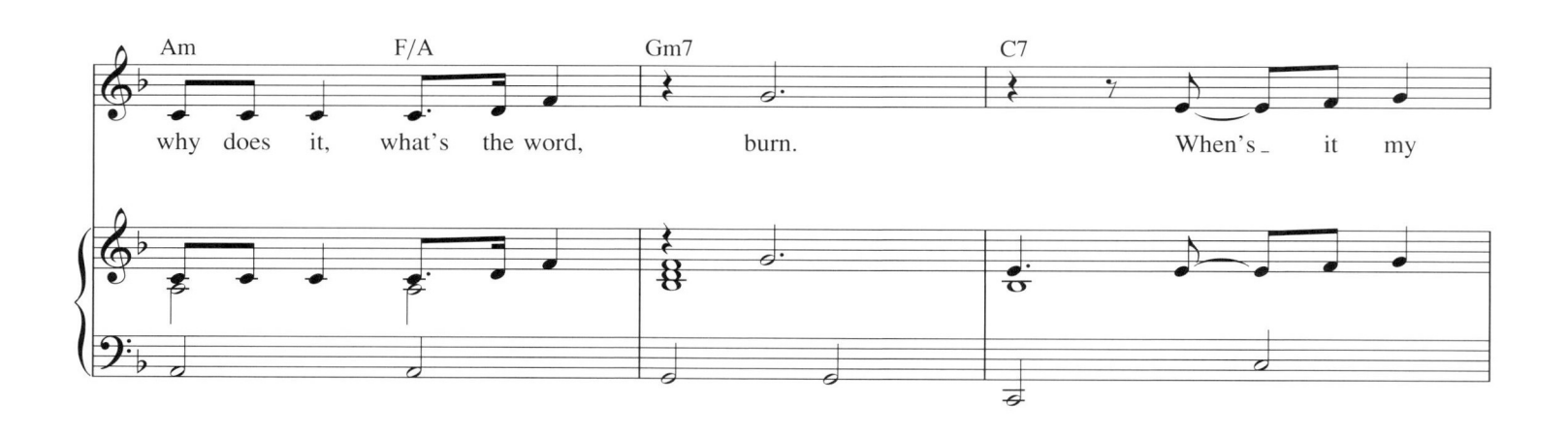

wom - en, sick of swim-min' read-y to stand. And read-y to know what the peo-ple know. Ask 'em my ques-tions and get some an-swers. What's a fire, and why does it, what's the word, burn. When's it my *turn? Would-n't I love, love to ex - plore that shore up a - bove, out of the sea. Wish I could be part of that world.*

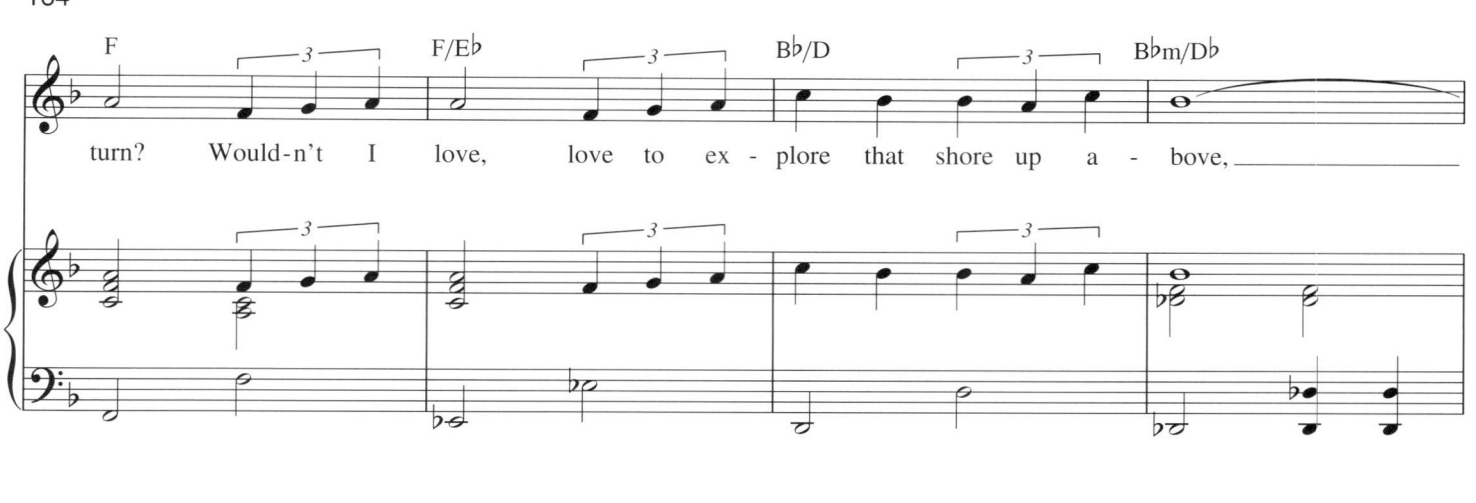

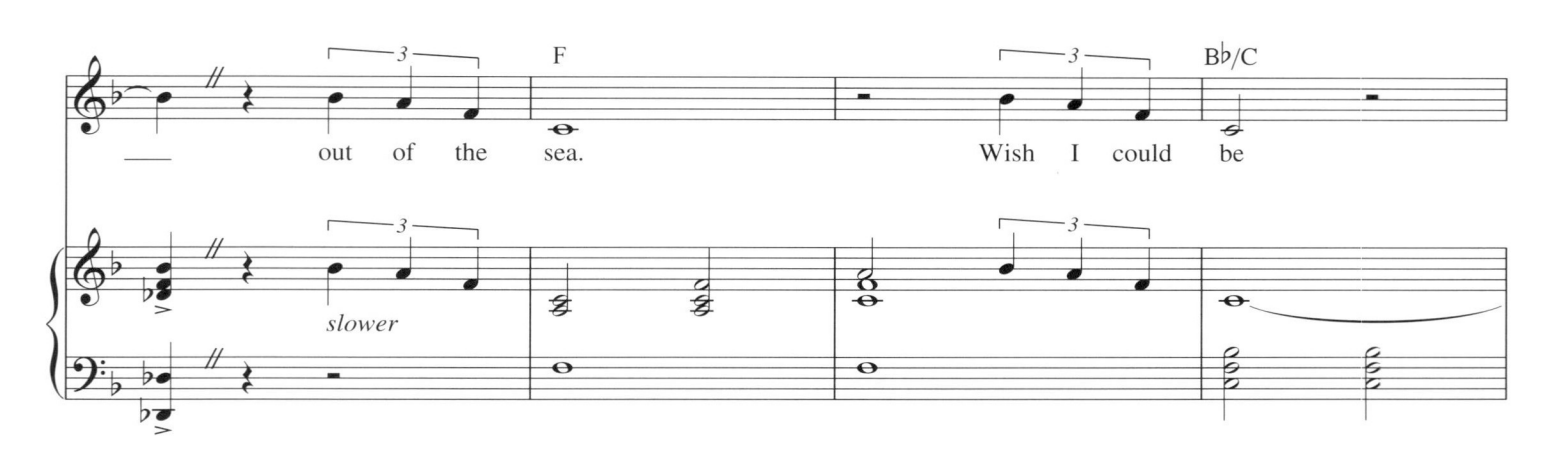

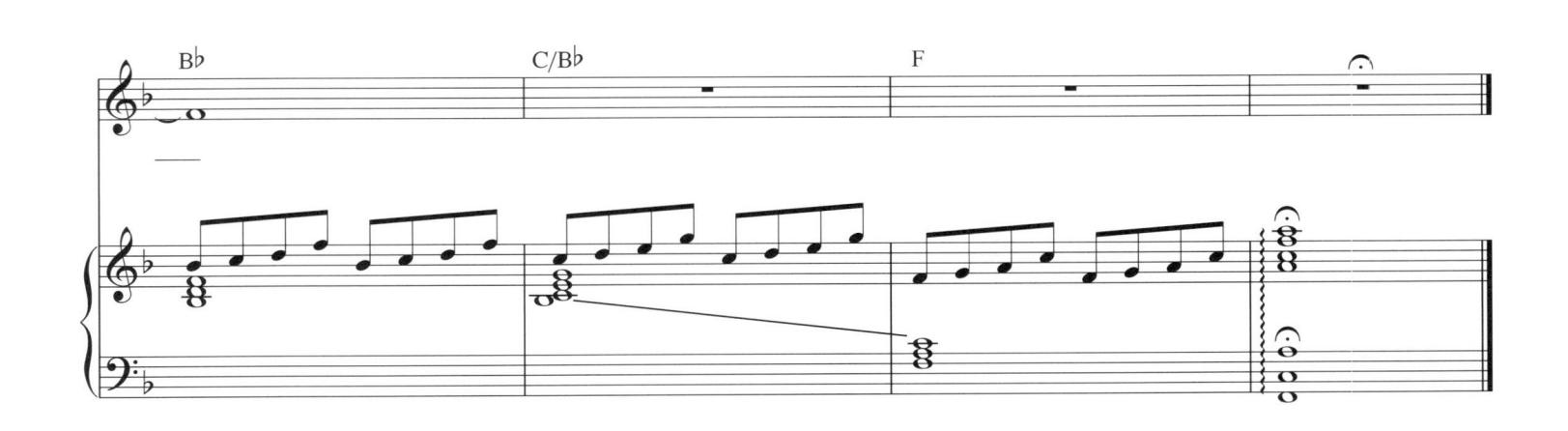

PUT ON A HAPPY FACE
from *Bye Bye Birdie*

Lyric by Lee Adams
Music by Charles Strouse

Rhythmically (lightly)

ALBERT:
Gray skies are gon-na clear up, ___ put on a hap-py face; Brush off the clouds and cheer up, ___ put on a hap-py face. Take off the gloom-y

mask of trag - e - dy, it's not your style; You'll look so good that you'll be glad ya' de - cid - ed to smile! Pick out a pleas - ant out - look, stick out that no - ble chin; Wipe off that "full of

Gm7(add11) C7 Fm7 B♭9 B♭m7 E♭7
doubt" look, slap on a hap - py grin! And
A♭maj7 Dm7♭5 E♭ Fm11 B♭7 G7♯5 G7 C9
spread sun - shine all o - ver the place, just
F13 B♭11 B♭13
opt.
1
E♭9 E♭6
put on a hap - py face!
Fm7 B♭7
2
E♭ E♭7 Fm7 E♭
face!

REAL LIVE GIRL
from *Little Me*

Music by Cy Coleman
Lyrics by Carolyn Leigh
Arranged by Michael Dansicker

Slow waltz tempo

Smooth, legato and square

FRED: Par-don, me miss, but I've nev-er done this with a real live girl. Straight off the farm with an ac-tu-al arm-ful of real live girl. Par-don me if your af-

Copyright © 1962 Notable Music Company, Inc. and EMI Carwin Music Inc.
Copyright Renewed
All Rights for Notable Music Company, Inc. Administered by Chrysalis Music
All Rights Reserved   Used by Permission

fec-tion-ate squeeze Fogs up my gog-gles and buck-les my knees.

I'm sim-ply drowned in the sight and the sound and the scent _____ and the

feel _____ of a real _____ live _____

girl. _____

Stronger - faster

Nothing can beat getting swept off your feet by a real live girl.

Dreams in your bunk don't compare with a hunk of a real live girl.

Speaking of miracles,

this must be it, Just when I start-ed to learn how to knit. I'm all in stitch-es from find-ing what rich-es a waltz can re-veal with a real live girl!

REFLECTION
from Walt Disney Pictures' *Mulan*

Music by Matthew Wilder
Lyrics by David Zippel

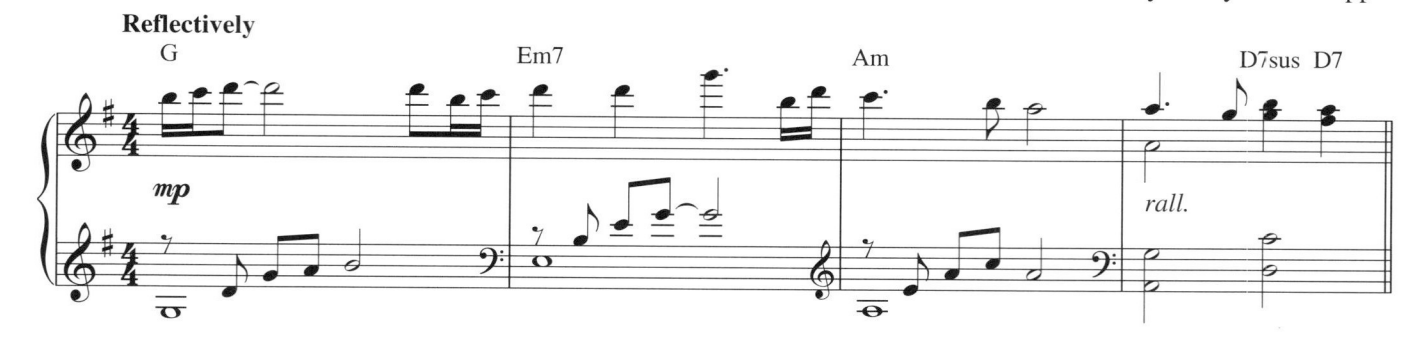

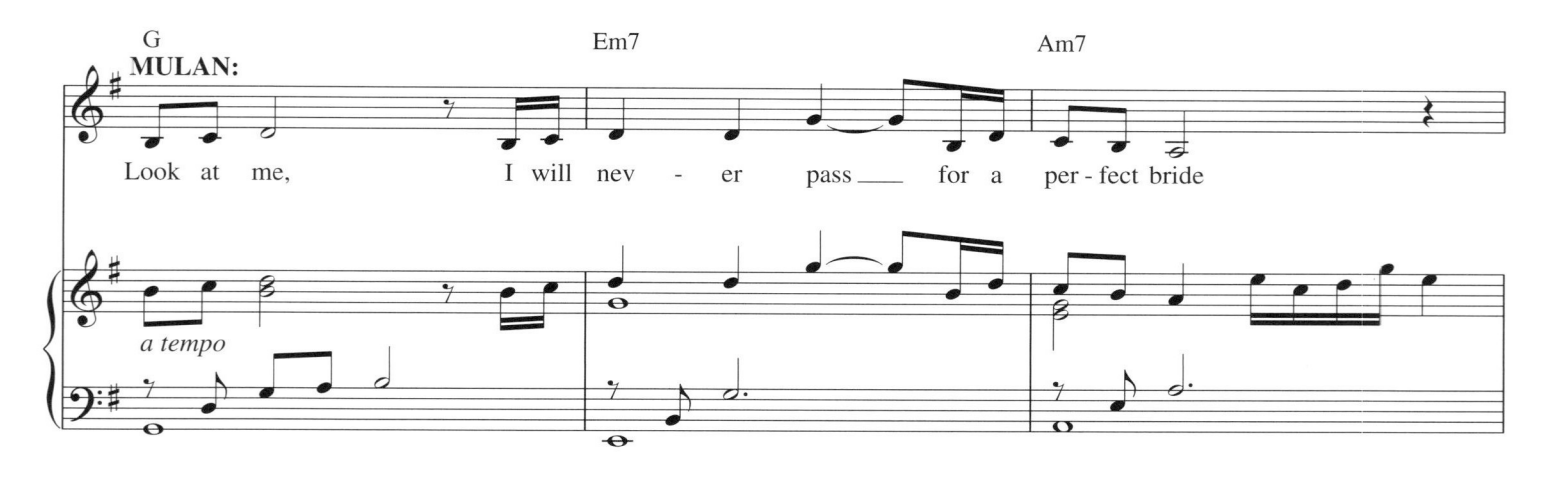

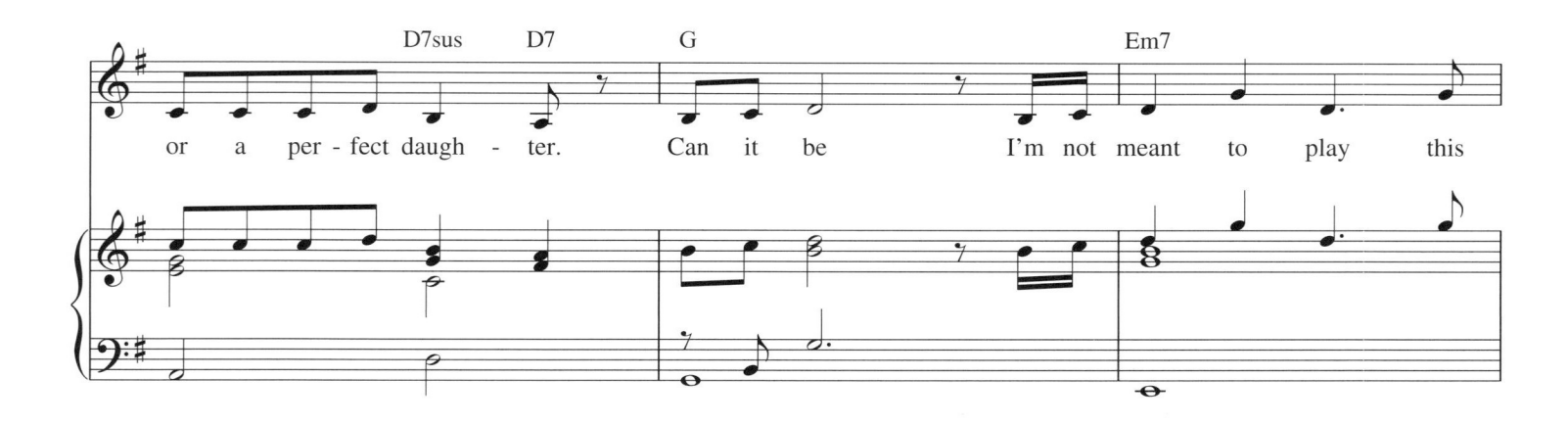

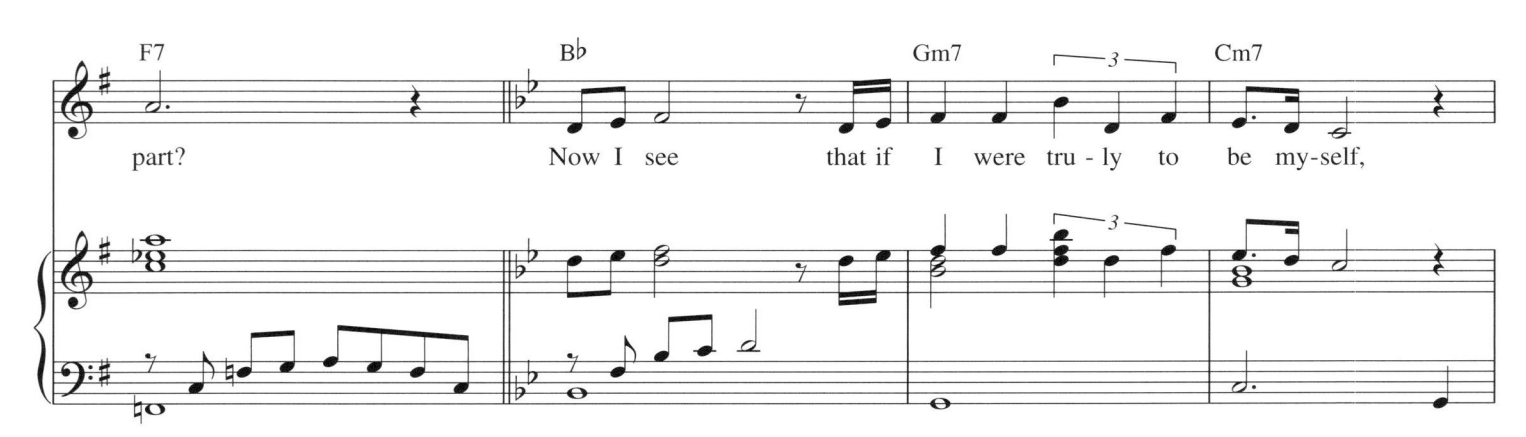

Reflectively

MULAN:
Look at me, I will nev-er pass___ for a per-fect bride or a per-fect daugh-ter. Can it be I'm not meant to play this part? Now I see that if I were tru-ly to be my-self,

© 1998 Walt Disney Music Company
All Rights Reserved Used by Permission

Cm7♭5
I would break my fam - 'ly's heart.
B♭
B♭(add9) B♭ Gm7 F/E♭ E♭
Who is that girl I see star - ing straight
E♭m(add9) B♭ F/A Gm7 Gm/F E♭maj7 A♭
back at me? Why is my re - flec - tion some - one I don't
F B♭(add9) Gm7
know? Some - how I can not hide

F/E♭ E♭ E♭m6 B♭ F/A Gm7 Gm/F
who I am, though I've tried. When will my re -
E♭maj9 E♭6 Gm Gm/F Gm/E
flec - tion show who I am in - side?
rit.
Slower
B♭ F/A Gm7 Gm/F E♭maj9 E♭m6
When will my re - flec - tion show who I am in -
rall.
E♭ Gm7 B♭(add9)
side?
a tempo

SING

from the Television Series *Sesame Street*

Words and Music by
Joe Raposo

Moderately

Sing! Sing a song. Sing out loud, sing out strong. Sing of good things not bad; sing of hap-py not sad. Sing! Sing a

Copyright © 1971 Jonico Music, Inc.
Copyright Renewed
All Rights in the U.S.A. Administered by Green Fox Music, Inc.
International Copyright Secured   All Rights Reserved

song. Make it simple to last your whole life long.

Don't worry that it's not good enough for anyone else to hear.

Sing! Sing a song!

La la do la da, La da la do la da, La da da la do la da.

177

La do la da, La da la la da, Lo da da la do lo da.

La la do la da, La da la do la da, La da da la do la da.

La la do la da, La da la do la da, La da da la do la da.

La la do la da, La da la do la da, La da da la do la da.

SO THIS IS LOVE
(The Cinderella Waltz)
from Walt Disney's *Cinderella*

Words and Music by Mack David,
Al Hoffman and Jerry Livingston

This song is performed by Cinderella and Prince Charming in the film, adapted here as a solo.

© 1948 Walt Disney Music Company
Copyright Renewed
All Rights Reserved Used by Permission

179

B♭
Gm7 C7 Gm7 Gm9 C9
sky. So this is the mir - a - cle that
eyes. You are the mir - a - cle
F Am7 D7 Gm7 C9 Gm7 C7♭9
I've been dream-ing of, so this is love, mm so this is
I've been dream-ing of,
1
F B♭/F F B♭/F
love. So this is
2
F Dm7 Gm7 F
love.
pp

THE UGLY DUCKLING
from the Motion Picture *Hans Christian Andersen*

By Frank Loesser

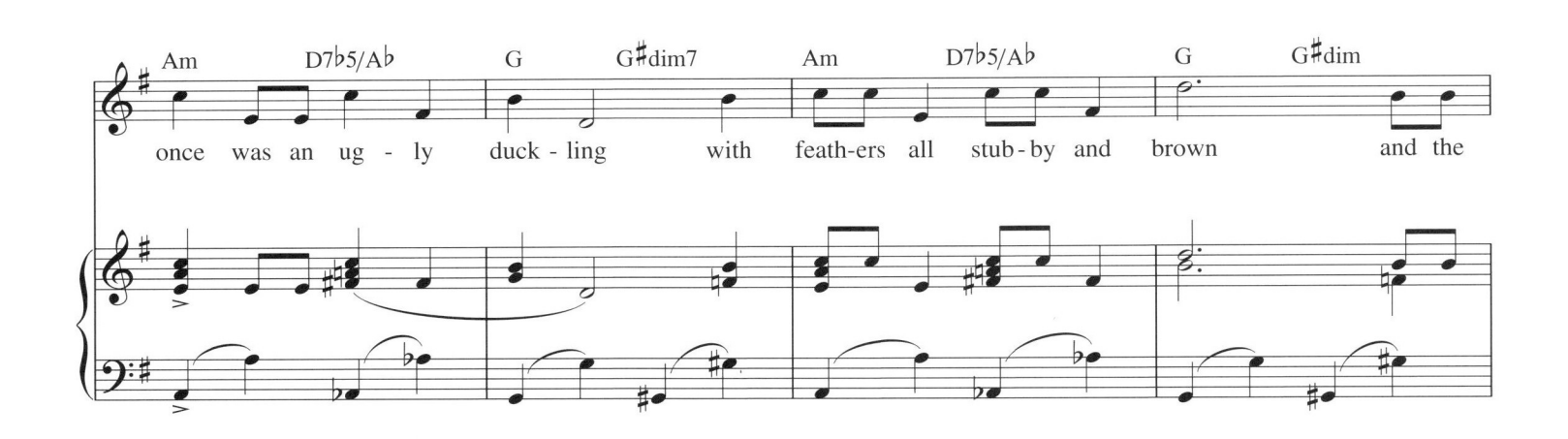

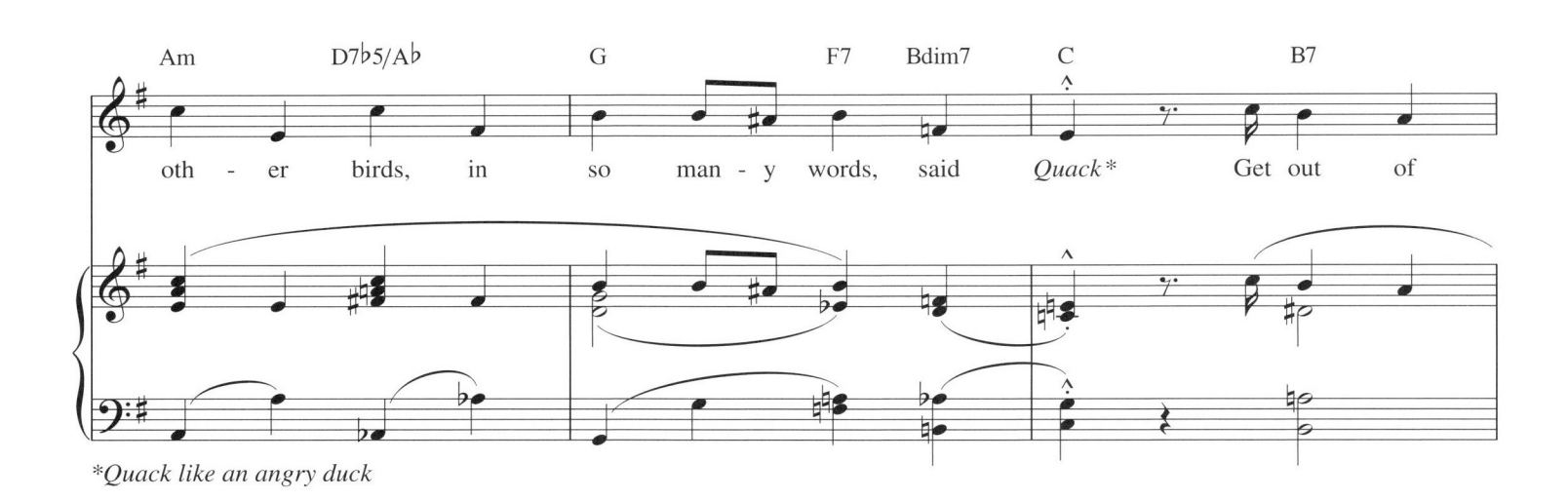

Lightly, with a waddle

HANS: There once was an ug-ly duck-ling with feath-ers all stub-by and brown and the oth-er birds, in so man-y words, said *Quack** Get out of

**Quack like an angry duck*

© 1951, 1952 (Renewed) FRANK MUSIC CORP.
All Rights Reserved

town. *Quack* get out, *Quack* *Quack* get out, *Quack* *Quack* get out of town. And he went with a quack and a waddle and a quack in a flurry of Eider-down. That poor little ugly duckling went wan-der-ing far and near but at ev-'ry place they said to his face now

Quack get out of here *Quack* get out, *Quack Quack* get out, *Quack*

Quack get out of here. And he went with a quack and a

wad-dle and a quack and a ver-y un-hap-py tear.

All through the winter-time he hid himself away. A-shamed to show his face. A-fraid of what others might say. All through the winter in his lonely clump of weed 'Til a flock of swans spied him there and ver-y soon a-greed: "You're a ver-y fine swan in-deed!" *(Spoken:)* "Swan? Me a swan? Aw go on!" "You're a swan! Take a look at your-self in the lake and you'll see!" And he looked and he saw, and he said, "Why, it's me! I

*Or whistle admiringly

quack, not a quack, not a wad-dle or a quack. But a glide and a whis-tle and a snow-y white back and a head so no-ble and high! Say, who's an ug-ly duck-ling? Not I _____ (Whistle or hum) (Sung:) Not I!

SOMEONE'S WAITING FOR YOU
from Walt Disney's *The Rescuers*

Words by Carol Connors and Ayn Robbins
Music by Sammy Fain

Ev-'ry child has man-y wish-es that they wish when they're a-lone. Faith can work just like mag-ic; noth-ing chang-es when you're grown. Be

© 1976 Walt Disney Music Company and Sammy Fain Trust
Copyright Renewed
Administered by Walt Disney Music Company
All Rights Reserved   Used by Permission

190

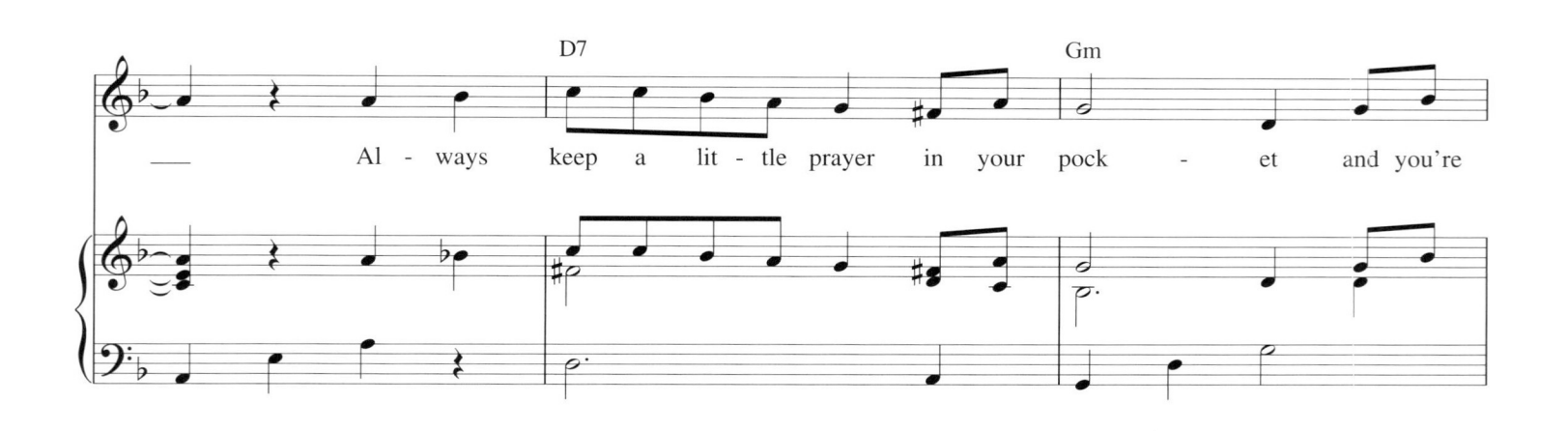

faith lit-tle one 'til your hopes and your wish-es come true

You must try to be brave lit-tle one_____ Some-one's

wait-ing to love you._____

TOMORROW
from the Musical Production *Annie*

Lyric by Martin Charnin
Music by Charles Strouse

ANNIE: The sun-'ll come out ____ to-mor-row, bet your bot-tom dol-lar that to-mor-row ____ there'll be sun! Jus' think-ing a-bout ____ to-mor-row

© 1977 (Renewed) EDWIN H. MORRIS & COMPANY, A Division of MPL Music Publishing, Inc. and CHARLES STROUSE
All rights on behalf of CHARLES STROUSE owned by CHARLES STROUSE PUBLISHING (Administered by WILLIAMSON MUSIC)
All Rights Reserved   Used by Permission
www.CharlesStrouse.com

clears a-way the cob-webs and the sor-row ___ till there's
none. When I'm stuck ___ with a day that's gray and
lone-ly, I just stick ___ out my chin and grin and
say: ___ Oh! the

F Fmaj7 B♭maj7 Am7
sun - 'll come out to - mor - row,
So you
Oh! I
got to hang on till to -
Dm Dm/C G♭maj7 C7sus C7
mor - row come what may! To -
1 (small notes are optional harmony)
F Fmaj7 F7 B♭ B♭m6
mor - row, to - mor - row, I love ya to - mor - row, you're
F C7sus C7 F Fmaj7 B♭maj7/F Gm7(add4)
al - ways
on - ly
a day a - way! The

mor - row, to - mor - row, I love ya to - mor - row, you're {always/only} a day a - way! To - mor - row, to - mor - row, I love ya to - mor - row, you're {always/only} a day a - way!

WE'RE ALL IN THIS TOGETHER

from the Disney Channel Original Movie *High School Musical*

Words and Music by Matthew Gerrard
and Robbie Nevil

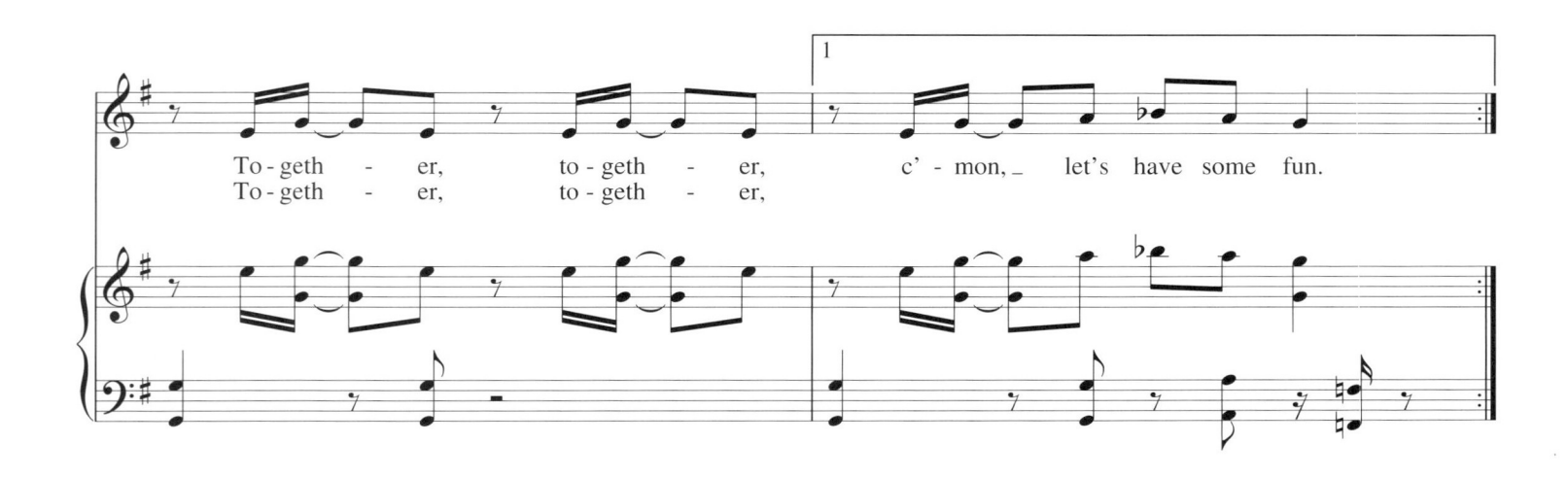

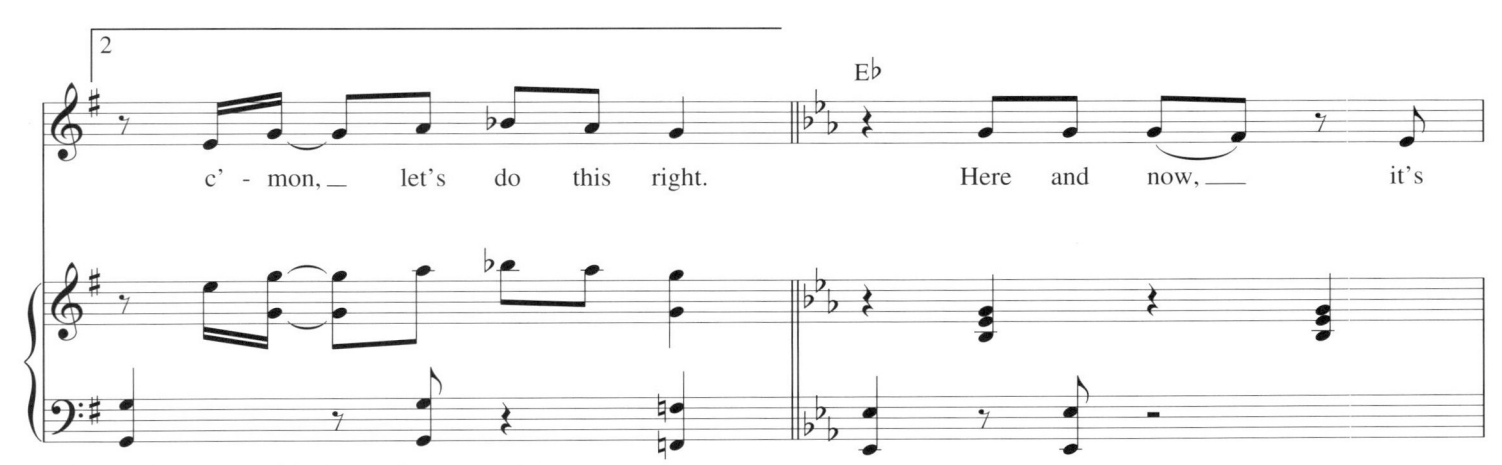

This song is an ensemble in the film, adapted here as a solo.

© 2005 Walt Disney Music Company
All Rights Reserved Used by Permission

time for cel-e-bra-tion. I fi-n'lly fig-ured out, yeah, yeah, that all our dreams have no lim-i-ta-tions; that's what it's all a-bout. (C'-mon, now.) Ev-'ry-one is spe-cial in their own way; we make each oth-er strong. We're not the same; we're diff'rent in a good way. To-geth-er's where we be-long. We're all in this to-geth-er; once we know that we are, we're all stars, and we see that. We're all in this to-geth-er; and it shows when we stand hand in hand, make our dreams come true.

G
Ev - 'ry - bod - y now: To - geth - er, to - geth - er,
To - geth - er, we're there _ for
F G
to - geth - er, ev - 'ry - one. To - geth - er, to - geth - er,
each oth - er ev - 'ry time. To - geth - er, to - geth - er,
1 F
c' - mon, _ let's have some fun.
2 F
c' - mon, _ let's do this right. We're
G D/F♯ Em G/D C G/B
all in this _ to - geth - er; once _ we know that we are, we're all stars,
all in this _ to - geth - er; when _ we reach, we can fly, know in - side

C/E D/F♯ G D/F♯ Em G/D
and we see that. We're all in this to-geth - er; and it shows
we can make it. We're all in this to-geth - er; once we see
C G/B
when we stand hand in hand,
there's a chance that we have,
1
C/E D/F♯
make our dreams come... We're
2
C/E D/F♯
and we take it.
F
Wild cats ev - 'ry - where, wave your hands up in the air.
That's the way we do it; let's get to it, c' - mon ev - 'ry - one!
G

WHEN YOU WISH UPON A STAR
from Walt Disney's *Pinocchio*

Words by Ned Washington
Music by Leigh Harline

who you are, An-y-thing your heart de-sires will come to you. If your heart is in your dream, no re-quest is too ex-treme, When you wish up-on a star as dream-ers do. Fate is kind, She brings to those who love, the sweet ful-fill-ment of their se-cret long-ing. Like a bolt out of the blue, Fate steps in and sees you thru, When you wish up-on a star your dream comes true. dream comes true.

WHEN I SEE AN ELEPHANT FLY
from Walt Disney's *Dumbo*

Words by Ned Washington
Music by Oliver Wallace

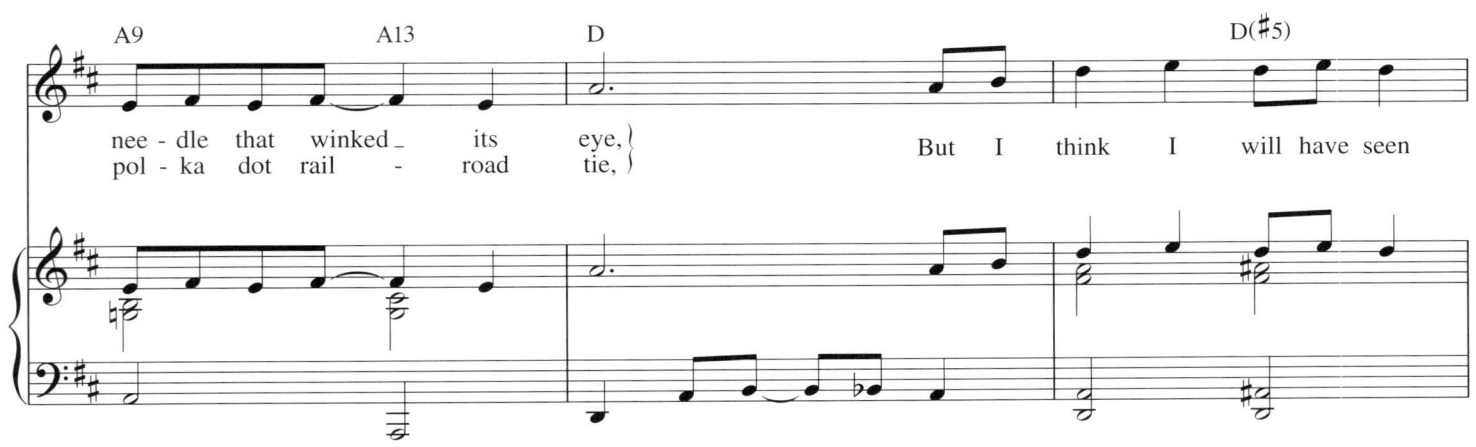

With a beat

I saw a pea-nut stand, heard a rub-ber band, I saw a nee-dle that winked its eye,
I saw a front porch swing, heard a dia-mond ring, I saw a pol-ka dot rail-road tie,

But I think I will have seen

This song is performed by The Crows in the film, adapted here as a solo.

Copyright © 1941 by Walt Disney Productions
Copyright Renewed
World Rights Controlled by Bourne Co. (ASCAP)
International Copyright Secured   All Rights Reserved

ev-'ry-thing when I see an el-e-phant fly. I saw a fly. I e-ven heard a choc-o-late drop, I went in-to a store, saw a bi-cy-cle shop. You can't de-ny the things that you see, But

I know there's cer-tain things that just can't be. The oth-er day by chance, saw an old barn dance, And I just laughed till I thought I'd die But I think I will have seen ev-'ry-thing When I see an el-e-phant fly.

YOU'RE NEVER FULLY DRESSED WITHOUT A SMILE

from the Musical Production *Annie*

Lyrics by Martin Charnin
Music by Charles Strouse
Arranged by Michael Dansicker

Not too fast

ANNIE:
Hey, ho-bo man, hey, Dap-per Dan, You've both got your style, But broth-er, you're nev-er ful-ly dressed with-out a smile. Your clothes may be

© 1977 (Renewed) EDWIN H. MORRIS & COMPANY, A Division of MPL Music Publishing, Inc. and CHARLES STROUSE
Worldwide publishing on behalf of CHARLES STROUSE owned by CHARLES STROUSE PUBLISHING (Administered by WILLIAMSON MUSIC)
All Rights Reserved   Used by Permission
www.CharlesStrouse.com

Beau Brum-mel-ly, They stand out a mile, But broth-er, you're never ful-ly dressed with-out a smile! Who cares what they're wear-ing on Main Street or Sa-ville Row? It's what you wear from ear to ear And not from head to toe, that mat-ters.

Stronger

So Senator, So janitor, So long for a while. Remember you're never fully dressed 'Tho' you may wear your best, You're never fully dressed without a smile, Smile, Smile, Smile, darn ya, smile!

WHERE IS LOVE?
from the Broadway Musical *Oliver!*

Words and Music by
Lionel Bart

Slowly, but rhythmically

OLIVER:
Where is love? Does it fall from skies a-bove?
Is it un-der-neath the wil-low tree that I've been dream-ing of?
Where is she, who I close my eyes to see? Will I ev-er know the

© Copyright 1960 (Renewed) and 1968 (Renewed) Lakeview Music Co. Ltd., London, England
TRO - HOLLIS MUSIC, INC. New York, controls all publication rights for the USA and Canada
International Copyright Secured   Made in USA
All Rights Reserved Including Public Performance For Profit

*In the film, Oliver sings the italicized lyrics the second time.

Dm
Gm7 A7 Dm
Who will tie it up with a rib - bon, and
Gm7 Gm7/C F
put it in a box for me?
So I can
There'll nev - er
Gm Gm7 C7♭9 Fmaj7 F6 F F6
see it at my lei - sure when -
be a day so sun - ny; it
Gm Gm7 C7♭9 Fmaj7 F6
ev - er things go wrong, and I would
could not hap - pen twice. Where is the

Am7 C/G F#m7b5 B7b9 Em
keep it as a treas - ure to
man with all the mon - ey? It's
Am Am/G F7 E7#5 A7b9 A7 A7b9 A7
last my whole life long.
cheap at half the price!
Dm Gm7 A7 Dm
Who will buy this won - der - ful feel - ing?
Gm7 Em7 A
I'm so high, I swear I could fly.

Me, oh, my, I don't want to lose it, so what am I to do, to keep the sky so blue? There must be some-one who will buy.

buy.

WITH A SMILE AND A SONG

from Walt Disney's *Snow White and the Seven Dwarfs*

Words by Larry Morey
Music by Frank Churchill

Moderately

SNOW WHITE:

With a smile and a song,
With a smile and a song,

Life is just like a bright sun-ny day, Your cares fade a-way,_____ And your heart is
All the world seems to wak-en a-new, Re-joic-ing with you,_____ As the song is

1. young.
2. sung.

Copyright © 1937 by Bourne Co. (ASCAP)
Copyright Renewed
International Copyright Secured   All Rights Reserved

E♭ E♭m B♭6 F7 B♭ B♭m
There's no use in grum-bling, When rain-drops come tum-bling, Re-
mf
C7 Cm7 F7
mem-ber you're the one, Who can fill the world with sun-shine.
decresc.
B♭ Gm7 Cm7 F7 B♭ Gm7 Cm7 F7
When you smile and you sing, Ev-'ry-thing is in tune and it's spring and
mp
B♭ B♭7/A♭ E♭/G F7 B♭6
rit.
life flows a-long, With a smile and a song.
rit.

THE WORK SONG
from Walt Disney's *Cinderella*

Words and Music by Mack David,
Al Hoffman and Jerry Livingston

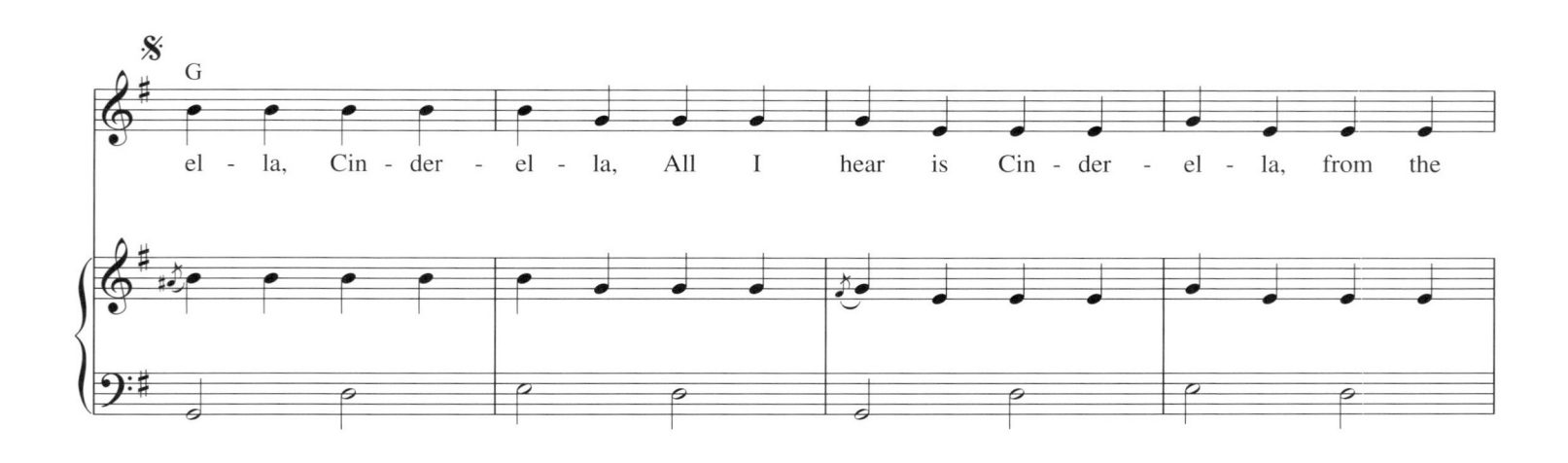

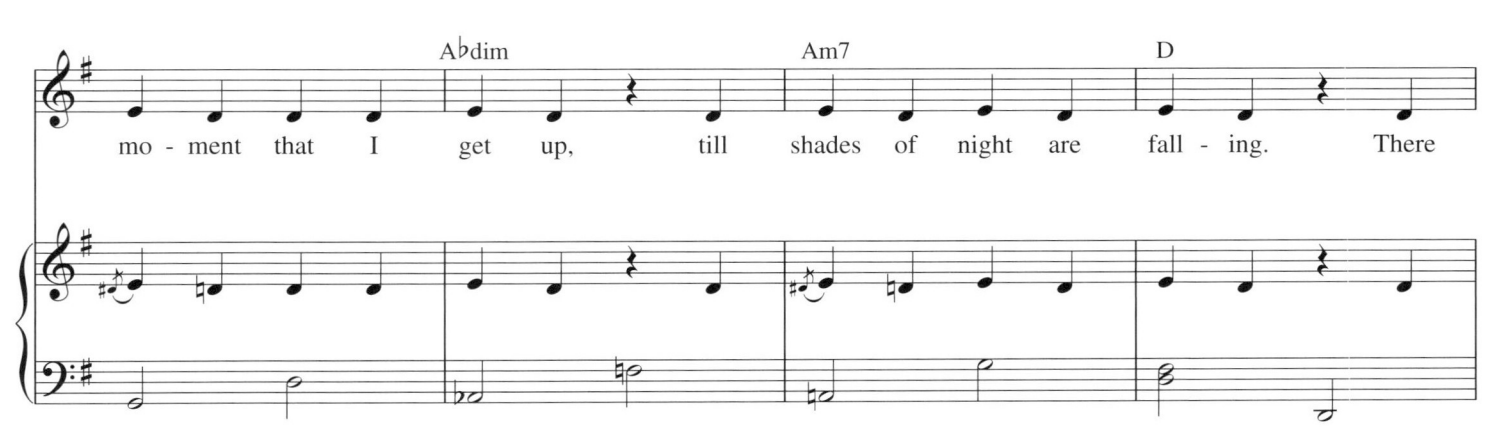

Brightly

Cin - der - el - la, Cin - der - el - la, All I hear is Cin - der - el - la, from the mo - ment that I get up, till shades of night are fall - ing. There

This song is performed by The Mice in the film, adapted here as a solo.

© 1948 Walt Disney Music Company
Copyright Renewed
All Rights Reserved   Used by Permission

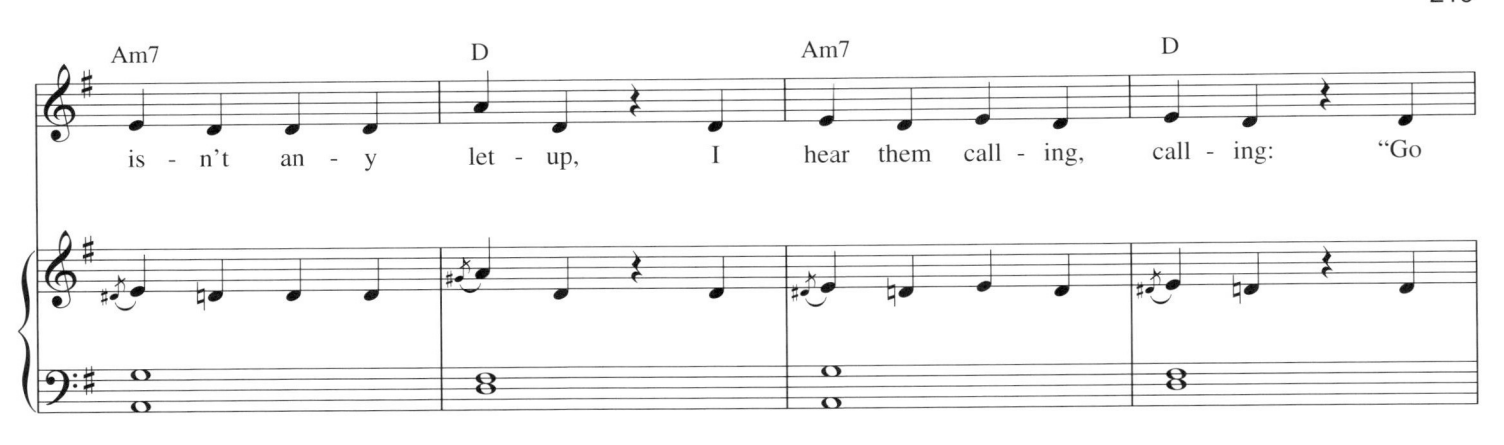

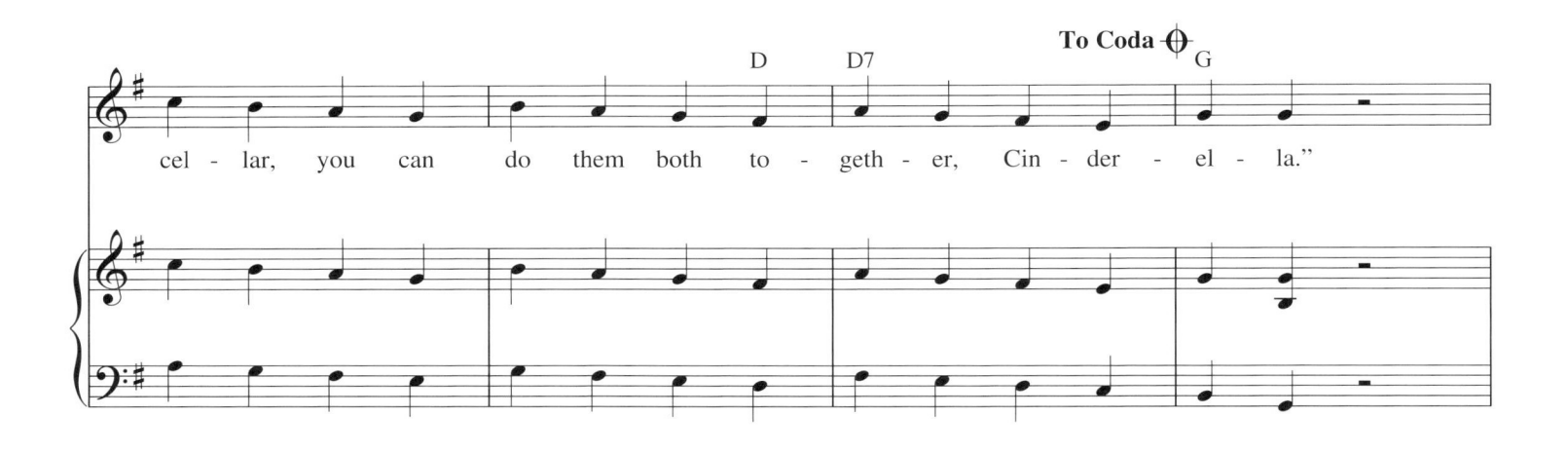

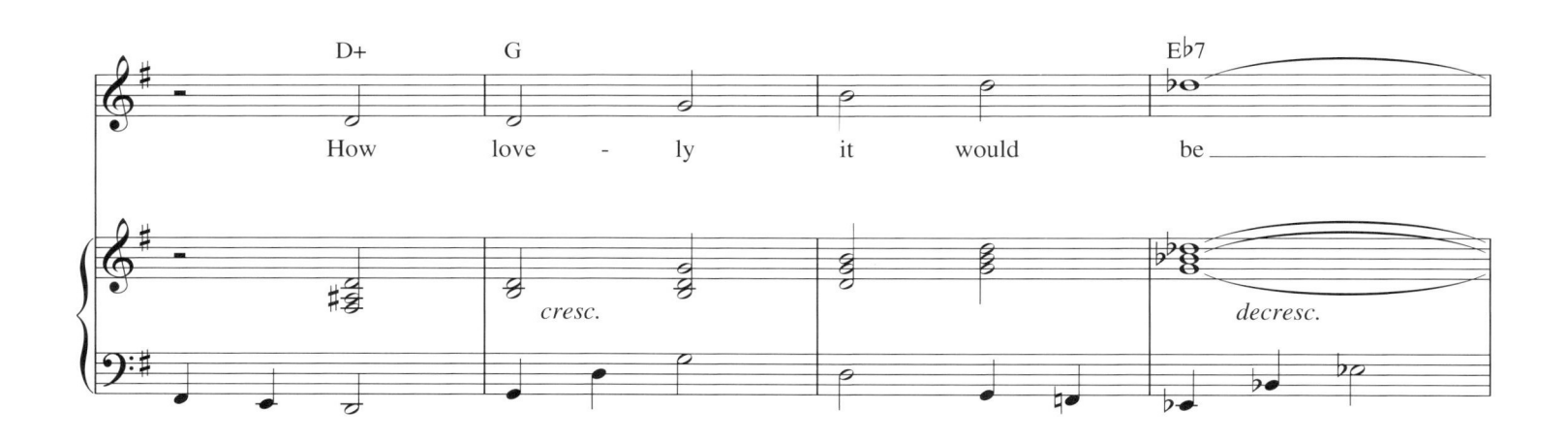

isn't an-y let-up, I hear them call-ing, call-ing: "Go up and do the at-tic and go down and do the cel-lar, you can do them both to-geth-er, Cin-der-el-la."

How love-ly it would be

if I could live my fan - ta - sy.

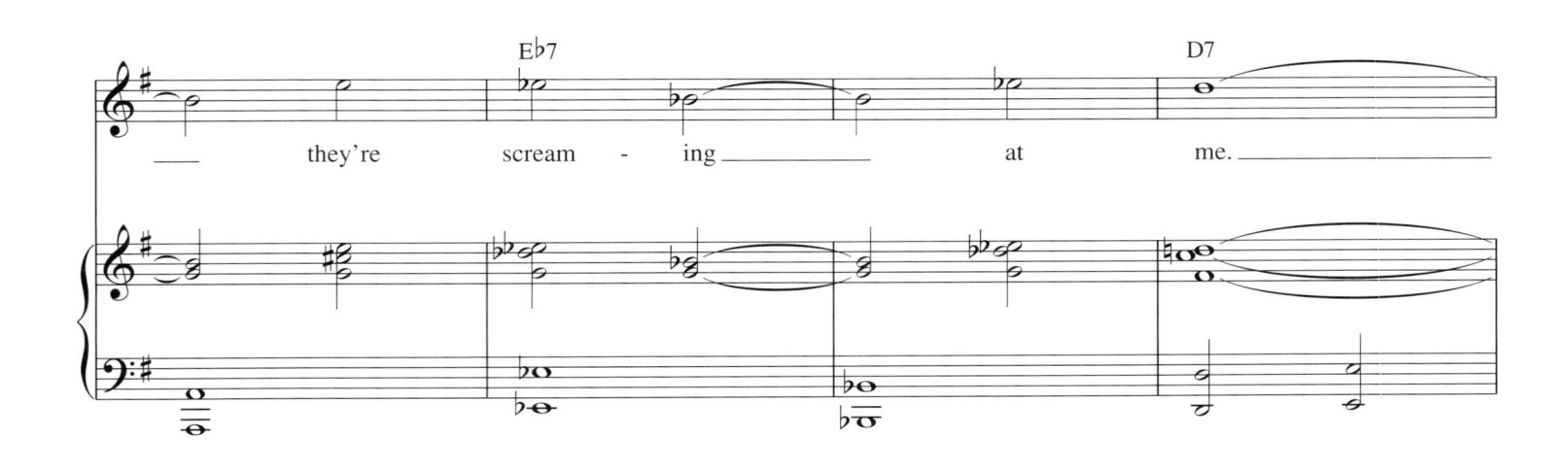

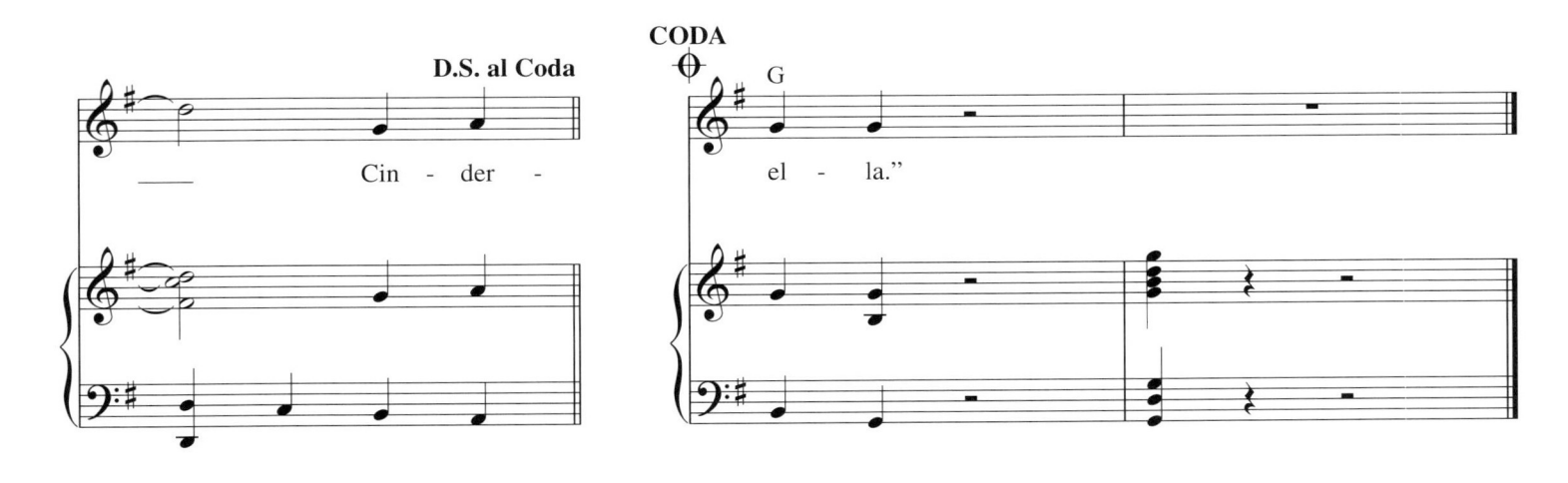

But in the mid - dle of my dream - ing

they're scream - ing at me.

D.S. al Coda

Cin - der -

CODA

el - la."

ZIP-A-DEE-DOO-DAH
from Walt Disney's *Song of the South*

Words by Ray Gilbert
Music by Allie Wrubel

Merrily

UNCLE REMUS:
Zip - a - dee - doo - dah, zip - a - dee - ay, My, oh, my, what a won - der - ful day!

© 1945 Walt Disney Music Company
Copyright Renewed
All Rights Reserved   Used by Permission

Plen - ty of sun - shine head - in' my way,

Zip - a - dee - doo - dah, zip - a - dee - ay!

Mis - ter Blue - bird on my shoul - der,

it's the truth, it's "act - ch'll,"

F N.C.
Bb F7 Bb
Ev - 'ry - thing is "sat - is - fact - ch'll." Zip - a - dee - doo - dah,
decresc.
mf
Eb Bb Eb Bb
zip - a - dee - ay! Won - der - ful feel -
Gm C7 F7 Bb
- ing, won - der - ful day. Mis - ter
1
mp
2
C F7 Bb
won - der - ful day.
f

WOULDN'T IT BE LOVERLY
from *My Fair Lady*

Words by Alan Jay Lerner
Music by Frederick Loewe

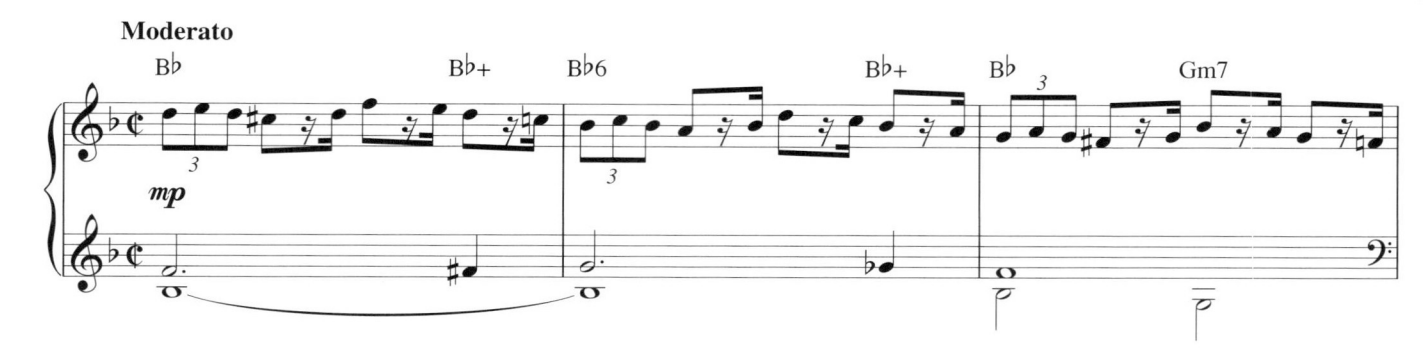

ELIZA: All I want is a room somewhere, Far away from the cold night air, With one e-

This song is performed by Eliza Doolittle and Cockneys in the show, adapted here as a solo.

© 1956 (Renewed) ALAN JAY LERNER and FREDERICK LOEWE
All Rights Administered by CHAPPELL & CO., INC.
All Rights Reserved   Used by Permission

nor - mous chair; Oh, would - n't it be lov - er - ly?

Lots of choc' - late for me to eat; Lots of coal mak - in'

lots of heat; Warm face, warm hands, warm feet, Oh,

would - n't it be lov - er - ly? Oh, so

lov - er - ly sittin' ab - so - bloom - in' - lute - ly still! I would nev - er budge 'til spring crept o - ver the win - dow - sill. Some - one's head rest - in' on my knee; Warm and ten - der as he can be; Who takes good care of me. Oh, would-n't it be lov-er-ly? lov-er-ly? Lov-er-ly! Lov-er-ly! Lov-er-ly! Lov-er-ly!

YOU'VE GOT A FRIEND IN ME

from Walt Disney's *Toy Story*

Music and Lyrics by
Randy Newman

© 1995 Walt Disney Music Company
All Rights Reserved Used by Permission

F C/E E7 Am
and miles from your nice warm bed,
There is-n't an-y-thing I would-n't do for you.
F B/F♯ C/G E/G♯ Am F7 E Am D7 G7
you just re-mem-ber what your old pal said. Son, you've got a friend in me.
If we stick to-geth-er we can see it through, 'cause you've got a friend in me.
C A7 D7 G7
Yeah, you've got a friend in me.
Yeah, you've got a friend in me.
1
C E7/B
Am A♭7 C/G Cdim/G G7

Now, some oth-er folks might be a lit-tle bit smart-er than I am, big-ger and strong-er too. May-be. But none of them will ev-er love you the way I do, just me and you, boy. And as the years go by, our friend-ship will nev-er die.

C/G C F F♯dim7 C/G E7/G♯ Am
You're gon - na see it's our des - ti - ny.
molto rit.
D7 G7 C A7 D7 G7
You've got a friend in me.
You've got a friend in me.
a tempo
C A7 D7 G7 C E7/B
You've got a friend in me.
3
Am A♭7 C/G Cdim/G G7 C
rit.